The Parent-Child
PLAYBOOK
Learning Activities for Building a Creative Mind

Dr. Richie
Educational psychologist

*To every parent striving to create moments of love, learning, and laughter–**you are your child's greatest gift.***

PROLOGUE

Parenting comes with moments of pure joy and discovery, but let's face it—playing with kids can be tough. Many parents feel unsure of how to connect with their children through play. What games should we play? What will actually help them grow? I've wrestled with these same questions as a parent myself. Even in my professional role as a learning psychologist, I've seen teachers, caregivers, and fellow parents struggle with the same concerns.

Play is so much more than entertainment—it's the foundation of a child's emotional, cognitive, and social development. Yet, in our fast-paced, digitally saturated lives, finding meaningful, enriching activities can feel overwhelming. That's why I created this workbook: to empower you with playful, research-backed ways to connect with your child and help them thrive.

This book is not just a list of activities—it's a guide to turning everyday moments into opportunities for creativity, learning, and joy. Whether you're building towers, solving puzzles, or simply sharing a laugh, each chapter equips you with tools to nurture your child's imagination, critical thinking, emotional intelligence, and more.

No one has all the answers, but together, we can embrace the beauty of parenting with curiosity and love. Let's play, grow, and discover the extraordinary potential in every small moment. This is your invitation to transform ordinary playtime into extraordinary memories.

Dr. Richie

HOW TO USE THIS BOOK

1. Start Anywhere: You don't need to read this book from cover to cover. Find the section that best aligns with your current parenting goals or your child's developmental needs, and focus on that.

2. Target Developmental Areas: If you're looking to support a specific aspect of your child's growth–whether it's emotional, cognitive, or physical–look for activities designed for that particular domain.

3. Feel Free to Adapt: While the activities are designed to guide you, feel free to modify them based on your child's preferences and personality. The suggested activities are flexible and can be personalized.

4. Use the Book as a Resource: Think of this book as a resource you can return to whenever needed. As your child grows and their needs evolve, you can revisit different sections to find new ways to engage with them.

5. Be Present and Engaged: The activities are designed to be interactive, so make sure to actively engage with your child during playtime. Your involvement is key to creating a positive and developmental experience.

6. Focus on One Activity at a Time: Don't feel the need to rush through the activities. Pick one activity at a time and give it your full attention. This allows both you and your child to fully benefit from the experience.

7. Monitor Progress: Keep track of your child's response to each activity. Some activities may be more effective than others, and by observing their reactions, you can adjust accordingly.

8. Adjust for Different Ages: The activities are suitable for a wide age range, so feel free to adapt them based on your child's stage of development. What works for a toddler may need to be modified for an older child.

9. Incorporate Play into Daily Life: The best way to make the most of these activities is to integrate them into your child's daily routine. Use everyday moments as opportunities for learning and bonding.

10. Reflect and Enjoy the Process: Take time to reflect on how each activity benefits your child. Remember, the goal is not just to complete activities, but to enjoy the moments of connection and growth together.

"One Day, Day One, Your Choice"

Table of Contents

1. Creativity and Imagination

Children are natural creators, constantly exploring and reimagining the world around them. This chapter celebrates their boundless potential, offering activities designed to spark originality and inventive thinking. By nurturing creativity and imagination, parents can help children develop problem-solving skills, resilience, and a lifelong love of learning. These moments of play not only bring joy but also lay the foundation for innovation and adaptability in their future endeavors.

"Wisdom begins in wonder." - *Socrates*

1. MAGICAL POTION LAB

Objective:

Create a magical potion lab experience where your child can explore creativity, cause-and-effect, and early science concepts through colorful, fizzy, and fantastical experiments.

Activity Overview:

In this activity, you and your child will become wizards or magical scientists, creating bubbling potions with colorful reactions. You'll mix simple ingredients like baking soda and vinegar, but with a fun, magical twist. The fizzy reactions, sparkling colors, and imaginative stories you create will spark curiosity and wonder. Your child will feel like a true alchemist, making potions that can cure dragons, make flowers bloom, or even put a sleep spell on mischievous elves!

What My Child Learns from This:

• Cause and Effect: Your child will see firsthand how different ingredients react with each other. They'll learn that adding vinegar to baking soda creates fizz, while food coloring turns the potion into their desired magical hue.

• Creativity and Imagination: Mixing different ingredients and crafting stories around each potion encourages imaginative thinking.

• Early Science Concepts: This activity introduces basic chemistry and the concept of reactions in a hands-on, fun way.

• Sensory Exploration: Your child will engage their senses by observing colors, textures, sounds, and even smells (if you choose to add scents!).

Materials Needed (Consider listing options):

• Clear jars or cups (helps see the magic happen!)

• Baking soda

• White vinegar

• Food coloring (multiple colors for more fun!)

• Glitter, sequins, or small beads (these are the magical "ingredients")

• Measuring spoons or small scoops

• Dropper or pipette (for precise "magical" drops)

• Large tray or shallow bin (to catch any fizz that spills over)

• Optional: Scented oils (for magical potion scents), dish soap (for extra bubbles), kitchen spices (like cinnamon or paprika for added magical effects)

Step-by-Step Instructions:

1. Set the Magical Scene

• *Parent's Prompt: "Alright, little wizard, we've been called to create some magical potions! Some will make flowers bloom, others will wake up sleepy dragons. Let's see what we can brew today!"*

• Ask your child to choose a potion they want to create. Write fun names like "Dragon's Breath" or "Fairy Dust" on small pieces of paper to label the jars.

2. Create the Potion Base

• *Parent's Prompt: "What color do you think a dragon's potion should be? Let's make it really special!"*

• Fill the jars with water. Let your child add food coloring. Mix colors together for new hues. This is the perfect chance to ask: "What color do you think happiness looks like?" or "What color would make the flowers bloom faster?"

3. Add Magical Ingredients

• *Parent's Prompt: "Now let's add some magical ingredients. How about some unicorn dust or mermaid scales? Sprinkle the glitter into your potion!"*

• Let your child add baking soda to the water. Follow up by adding glitter or beads. Pretend these are magical creatures or powders that will make the potion even more powerful.

4. The Grand Reaction

• *Parent's Prompt: "Ready for the magical moment? Pour the vinegar in and let's see what happens!"*

• Slowly pour vinegar into each jar and watch the reaction. Ask your child to observe the fizz, foam, and bubbles. "Is this enough to wake the dragon, do you think?"

• Optional: Add dish soap for more bubbles or experiment with adding scented oils like lavender for a calming potion.

5. Creative Twist

• *Parent's Prompt: "Now, let's see if we can create a rainbow potion! We'll layer different colors. What do you think will happen when they mix?"*

• Try layering different colors and observe how they mix together. You can even make a challenge to see who can create the brightest potion!

6. Potion Debrief

• *Parent's Prompt: "What do you think your potion does? Could it help a princess sleep better, or maybe make someone laugh?"*

• After the reaction, ask your child to name their potion and describe its magical effects. This helps reinforce the creativity and storytelling aspect.

Reflective Questions to Deepen the Experience:

- *"What made the potion bubble so much? Why do you think that happened?"*
- *"How did the colors mix when you added the second one? What did you notice?"*
- *"What do you think your potion can do? Who would it help in a fairy tale world?"*
- *"If you could add one more ingredient, what would it be and why?"*
- *"How did it feel to make your own potion? Did you feel like a wizard?"*
- *"Do you think you could make a potion that would make flowers grow? How would you do that?"*
- *"What happens if we try a bigger or smaller amount of baking soda? Do you think the fizzing will change?"*
- *"Could we create a potion that smells like a sunny day or a spooky night?"*
- *"How can we use our potion ingredients in other ways? What if we mix them with other things we find in the house?"*
- *"What would happen if you mixed a potion for a dragon with one for a unicorn? What kind of magic would that create?"*

Bonus Challenges or Variations:

• Potion Sensory Challenge: Add essential oils or spices to give your potion a magical scent. Ask your child to guess what it smells like (e.g., "Does it smell like a wizard's lair or a forest full of fairies?").

• Potion Bottle Race: Who can make the most colorful and fizzy potion? Add a friendly competition for an extra twist!

• Potion Color Theory: Try making a "color wheel" potion where you create different colors by mixing primary colors (red, blue, yellow) and learn about color theory as you go!

• Seasonal Potions: Use different colors and scents that correspond to seasons (e.g., autumn potions with cinnamon and orange, or winter potions with peppermint and white glitter).

Why This Activity Matters:

This activity is designed to allow children to explore creativity, science, and imagination all while building a special memory with their parent. It's an exciting, hands-on experience that introduces basic scientific principles in an easy-to-understand, magical way. Not only does it promote exploration, but it also helps children build their own narratives and creative thoughts around the concept of cause and effect.

2. BUILD A DREAMLAND

Objective:

Help your child create their very own dream world, where imagination and creativity shape the landscape. This activity fosters spatial awareness, storytelling, and creative thinking as your child designs a fantastical world that reflects their interests and imagination.

Activity Overview:

In this activity, you and your child will use materials like blocks, fabric, paper, or any creative supplies you have on hand to build a dreamland. Your child can design everything from castles to forests, mystical creatures, and even entire cities. As you build, encourage your child to think about what their dream world looks like, who lives there, and how everything fits together. This activity nurtures problem-solving, storytelling, and fine motor skills as they arrange and construct their dreamland.

What Your Child Learns from This:

• Spatial Awareness: Building a dreamland involves understanding how different pieces fit together, promoting a sense of space and organization.

• Imagination and Creativity: Your child can bring their fantasy world to life, learning to express themselves through creative design and construction.

• Storytelling Skills: Encouraging your child to come up with stories about their dreamland strengthens narrative thinking and language development.

• Fine Motor Skills: Handling building materials, arranging objects, and creating detailed elements helps develop your child's fine motor control.

Materials Needed (Consider listing options):

• Building blocks (e.g., LEGO, wooden blocks, or cardboard boxes)

• Fabric pieces (to make "roads," "rivers," or "grass")

• Colored paper (for crafting trees, mountains, or creatures)

• Markers or crayons (for drawing details or creating characters)

• Stickers or stamps (to decorate and add fun details)

• Nature items (such as leaves, pebbles, or twigs for realism)

• Dollhouse furniture or action figures (to populate your dreamland)

• Scissors and glue (for crafting and assembling the dream world)

• Optional: Small figurines or plush toys to represent characters

Step-by-Step Instructions:

1. Set the Scene

• *Parent's Prompt: "Let's create a dreamland that's all yours! What do you think your dream world looks like? Do you want it to have a castle, a beach, or a magical forest?"*

• Ask your child to describe their dreamland. You can give prompts like, "What animals or people would live there?" or "Is there a big castle or a treehouse?"

2. Plan the Layout

• *Parent's Prompt: "How do you want your dreamland to be arranged? Should we start with the mountains and build up, or maybe start with the ocean and go from there?"*

• Help your child decide where to start building. Talk about the different "land features" they want in their world: rivers, mountains, deserts, and forests. Use blocks to sketch out the layout of the land.

3. Create the Buildings and Landmarks

• *Parent's Prompt: "What do you think your castle or treehouse would look like? Let's make it as big or small as you want!"*

• Work together to create the key landmarks in your dreamland, like a castle, a village, a mountain, or a bridge. Encourage your child to use their imagination and build structures out of whatever materials you have.

4. Add the Characters

• *Parent's Prompt: "Who will live in your dreamland? Maybe there's a queen, some fairies, or a dragon? Let's make some characters for your world!"*

• Help your child create characters or animals to populate their dreamland. They can make people out of paper or use toys to represent the inhabitants.

5. Decorate and Personalize

• *Parent's Prompt: "Now we get to decorate your dreamland. What colors will the sky be? Should there be stars at night or a rainbow in the sky?"*

• Use fabric, paper, or markers to add decorations like flowers, trees, clouds, or stars. Encourage your child to think about details like what the weather is in their dreamland and how it feels.

6. Tell the Story

• *Parent's Prompt: "Now that we've built your dreamland, let's make a story about it! What happens in this magical world? Who lives here and what do they do?"*

• Encourage your child to come up with a story about their dreamland. Ask them questions like: "What adventure would happen here?" or "Who would visit your dreamland?"

Reflective Questions to Deepen the Experience:

• *"What's the most important part of your dreamland? Why is that your favorite?"*

• *"What would you do if you lived in your dreamland? Who would you hang out with?"*

• *"Can you think of a way to make the dreamland even better? What else could we add?"*

• *"What kinds of adventures could happen in your dreamland? Would there be any challenges?"*

• *"Who would visit your dreamland? What would they do when they arrive?"*

• *"How does your dreamland look at night? Does it change when the sun sets?"*

• *"If you had to choose a magical creature to live in your dreamland, what would it be?"*

• *"How does your dreamland make you feel? Do you think it's a peaceful place or an exciting one?"*

• *"Can we make a map of your dreamland to show others? What's the most important part to include?"*

• *"How would you feel if you could step into your dreamland? Would you explore or relax?"*

Bonus Challenges or Variations:

• Dreamland Time Capsule: After creating the dreamland, draw a picture of it and write a small note about what you imagine life would be like in that world. Put it in a "time capsule" (like a small box) to open together in a few weeks and reflect on the changes or additions made.

• Dreamland Expansion: Encourage your child to keep adding to their dreamland over time. Create new sections or add new characters as their imagination grows. Turn it into an ongoing project where new areas of the world unfold.

• Building Challenge: For an added challenge, set up a "time limit" to build specific elements like a castle, forest, or garden. This can help your child think about how to organize their dreamland and problem-solve in a timed context.

Why This Activity Matters:

This activity is designed to encourage creativity, spatial reasoning, and storytelling. It's also a wonderful opportunity for bonding, as both you and your child work together to bring their imaginative world to life. Through building and reflecting on their dreamland, children will learn valuable skills that extend far beyond the world they create.

3. ADVENTURE IN A BOX

Objective:

Create an interactive and imaginative adventure for your child, all from the comfort of your own home. Through a "box of adventure," your child will embark on a journey of discovery, problem-solving, and creativity, using simple materials and their imagination to explore new worlds.

Activity Overview:

In this activity, you and your child will create an adventure that fits inside a box! Think of it as a mini world where your child is the explorer, and the box holds treasures, clues, and challenges. They'll use their imagination to discover what's inside and solve puzzles or face fun tasks along the way. This activity fosters problem-solving, creative thinking, and physical activity in a fun, engaging, and hands-on way.

What Your Child Learns from This:

• Imaginative Play: Your child will explore the concept of imaginative play as they build and navigate their own adventure.

• Problem-Solving Skills: As your child encounters puzzles, clues, or challenges, they'll learn how to think critically and find solutions.

• Spatial Awareness: Understanding how to arrange items in the box and how the "adventure" unfolds in real space helps children develop spatial thinking.

• Creative Thinking: Your child will be tasked with thinking outside the box (pun intended!) to create or solve various aspects of the adventure.

• Physical Activity: Many variations of the activity will involve movement, helping your child stay active and engaged while having fun.

Materials Needed (Consider listing options):

• A box (big enough to hold a few objects and allow room for exploration)

• Puzzles or clues (simple riddles, pictures, or challenges written on paper)

• Treasures (small toys, trinkets, or items that can be hidden in the box as rewards)

• Craft materials (e.g., colored markers, paper, stickers, or fabric to decorate the box and its contents)

• Maps or drawings (to create a "treasure map" or clues for the adventure)

• Props (e.g., small plush animals, plastic gems, or other objects to enhance the adventure theme)

• Optional: A blindfold for challenges that require extra sensory input

Step-by-Step Instructions:

1. Create the Adventure Map

• *Parent's Prompt: "Let's plan the greatest adventure ever! What kind of world do you want to explore today? A jungle filled with hidden treasures or maybe a secret underwater kingdom?"*

• Sit with your child and decide the theme of the adventure (e.g., pirates, explorers, or detectives). You can use simple paper or cardboard to draw a map or set up a series of clues.

2. Decorate the Box

• *Parent's Prompt: "Let's make our box look like the entrance to a secret world. What should we put on the outside to make it look mysterious?"*

• Let your child decorate the box with stickers, drawings, or objects that align with the adventure theme. This step adds a tactile and creative element to the activity.

3. Fill the Box with Treasures

• *Parent's Prompt: "Now, we'll hide some special treasures in the box. What would a pirate hide in their chest? Maybe a shiny gem or a secret map?"*

• Place small objects inside the box, such as small toys, colorful paper gems, or other items that can be found along the adventure. Make sure each item fits with the storyline you've decided on.

4. Set up Clues or Challenges

• *Parent's Prompt: "I think we need a secret code to open the treasure chest! Can you figure out what's hidden behind this clue?"*

• Create simple puzzles or clues (e.g., "Find the key under the jungle leaves!"). These clues can be riddles, pictures, or hidden messages. Tailor the difficulty of the clues based on your child's age and abilities.

5. The Adventure Begins!

• *Parent's Prompt: "Are you ready for the adventure? Let's go on a treasure hunt! Follow the map and see what you find next."*

• Have your child follow the clues, search for hidden items, and solve problems along the way. Let them discover the treasures, face challenges, and interact with the items you've placed in the box.

6. Reflection and Debrief

• *Parent's Prompt: "Wow! You did it! What was your favorite part of the adventure? What do you think we should add next time?"*

• After the adventure, sit down with your child to discuss what they found, what they liked about the activity, and what challenges they faced. This helps them reflect on their experience and think critically about their problem-solving.

Reflective Questions to Deepen the Experience:

• *"What part of the adventure was the hardest for you? How did you figure it out?"*

• *"How did you feel when you found the treasure?"*

• *"Do you think the clues helped you? What else could we do to make them trickier?"*

• *"If you were to make an adventure for someone else, what would it be like?"*

• *"What kind of clues do you think would be the most fun to hide in the box?"*

• *"What would happen if we added a twist to the adventure, like a surprise or an obstacle?"*

• *"What treasure would you want to hide in a box if you could?"*

• *"What could we add to the box to make it even more magical?"*

• *"If you could design an adventure map, what would it look like?"*

• *"Would you like to create a new story or theme for the next adventure?"*

Bonus Challenges or Variations:

• Time Challenge: Set a timer to see how fast your child can solve the puzzles and find all the treasures. Add a sense of urgency and excitement.

• Sensory Adventure: Close the box and have your child find treasures by touch alone (blindfolded or with the lid closed). This challenge encourages sensory development.

• Nature Hunt: If you have access to a garden or outdoor area, hide "treasures" like leaves, rocks, or natural objects in the box. This variation helps incorporate nature into the activity.

• Team Adventure: Create a box of adventures for multiple children. They can work together as a team to solve the puzzles and complete the mission.

Why This Activity Matters:

This "Adventure in a Box" activity offers a fun and dynamic experience where your child can practice thinking, exploring, and creating. It's simple to set up but can be endlessly varied, making it a versatile and educational activity you can adapt to different ages and interests. Plus, it's a great way for parents to bond with their children while nurturing their imagination and problem-solving abilities.

4. CREATE YOUR SUPERHERO

Objective:

This activity encourages your child to step into the world of imagination, creativity, and self-expression by designing their own superhero. Through this fun exercise, they'll learn to think about their strengths, abilities, and the ways they can help others, all while practicing their storytelling skills.

Activity Overview:

In this activity, your child will create a superhero character, complete with unique powers, a special name, and an exciting backstory. They will think about their superhero's abilities, what makes them special, and how they would use their powers to make the world a better place. This process not only nurtures your child's creativity but also helps them develop a deeper understanding of self-expression, empathy, and personal strengths.

What Your Child Learns from This:

• Self-Discovery and Confidence: By designing a superhero with unique abilities, your child can reflect on their own qualities and strengths, fostering self-esteem and self-awareness.

• Creativity and Storytelling: Your child will engage in creative thinking by inventing their own superpowers, designing costumes, and building a compelling backstory.

• Problem-Solving and Empathy: They'll also think critically about how their superhero helps others, encouraging a mindset focused on helping and solving problems.

• Character Building: Through the process of naming and defining their superhero, children will practice important character-building skills like empathy, kindness, and leadership.

Materials Needed (Consider listing options):

• Paper or poster board (for drawing or writing)

• Markers, crayons, or colored pencils (for designing the superhero's costume and powers)

• Stickers or other embellishments (optional, for adding fun details to the superhero)

• A blank superhero template (optional, to guide the design of their superhero)

• A notebook or journal (for writing the superhero's story and backstory)

• Imagination! (the most important material!)

Step-by-Step Instructions:

1. Introduce the Superhero Theme

• *Parent's Prompt: "Today, we're going to create a superhero! What powers would you have if you could do anything? Would you fly like a bird or have super strength?"*

• Encourage your child to think about a superhero that reflects their personal dreams and desires. Discuss famous superheroes for inspiration, but let their imagination run wild!

2. Designing the Superhero

• *Parent's Prompt: "Now, let's create your superhero's look. What kind of costume would they wear? Would they have a cape? What colors do they like?"*

• Allow your child to draw or describe their superhero's outfit and special accessories. Discuss why they chose those colors or designs. Perhaps they want their superhero to have a symbol like a star or lightning bolt!

3. Create the Superhero's Powers

• *Parent's Prompt: "What superpowers would your superhero have? Can they control the weather, or maybe they can talk to animals? Let's think about what makes them unique."*

• Ask your child to think about how their superhero's powers can help others. They may have multiple powers, like being able to fly and heal people with a magical touch, or they may specialize in one superpower.

4. Build the Superhero's Story

• *Parent's Prompt: "Every superhero has a story. Where did your superhero come from? Did they get their powers from a magical artifact or from helping others?"*

• Help your child create a backstory for their superhero. Where do they live? Who do they help? What challenges have they faced? This is a chance to incorporate lessons on resilience, bravery, and kindness.

5. Name Your Superhero

• *Parent's Prompt: "What's your superhero's name? Maybe it's something like 'The Brave Guardian' or 'Lightning Star'. It should sound like they're unstoppable!"*

• Encourage your child to come up with a powerful and creative name that reflects the character's abilities and personality.

6. Superhero Adventure Time

• *Parent's Prompt: "Now that we know your superhero's powers, let's create an adventure. What happens when they use their powers for good? What villains or challenges do they face?"*

• Together, come up with an adventure for the superhero where they use their powers to save the day. This could be a simple story or even a role-playing game where your child acts out the superhero's actions.

Reflective Questions to Deepen the Experience:

• *"What makes your superhero different from other heroes? What do they do that no one else can?"*

• *"If your superhero had to save someone, who would they help and why?"*

• *"How would your superhero solve a big problem in the world? What powers would they use?"*

• *"Do you think your superhero would work alone, or would they have a team of other superheroes?"*

• *"What is your superhero's greatest fear or challenge? How do they overcome it?"*

• *"How does your superhero make the world a better place?"*

• *"What does your superhero do when they're not fighting villains or saving people?"*

• *"If you could give your superhero one more power, what would it be?"*

• *"What kind of villain would your superhero face? What is their mission?"*

• *"What is the most exciting part of being a superhero?"*

Bonus Challenges or Variations:

• Create a Sidekick: Design a superhero sidekick who works alongside your main hero. What powers would the sidekick have? What special role do they play in the adventures?

• Superhero Comic Book: After designing the superhero, help your child create a short comic book about their superhero's first adventure. Draw panels and write the script together!

• Superhero Mask Craft: For an added twist, create a superhero mask together out of craft supplies. Wear it while playing out superhero adventures.

• Superhero Collaboration: Team up with a friend or sibling to create a superhero duo or team, each with their own powers. What's the team's mission, and how do they work together?

Why This Activity Matters:

This activity is not only a creative outlet for children but also a wonderful opportunity for self-expression and storytelling. By crafting their own superhero, children can learn about the value of helping others, embrace their personal strengths, and tap into their imagination to create powerful, positive narratives. It's a fun and engaging way for children to explore both the world of heroes and their own potential!

5. CLOUD SCULPTURES

Objective:

This activity allows your child to tap into their creativity and imagination while exploring the wonders of nature. Together, you'll craft cloud sculptures using cotton balls and other materials, helping your child learn about shapes, textures, and the concepts of clouds, weather, and the sky.

Activity Overview:

Cloud Sculptures is an imaginative, hands-on activity where children can recreate the fluffy, ever-changing shapes of clouds. By using cotton balls and crafting supplies, your child will create their own version of clouds that reflect the beauty of the sky. This activity not only engages their creativity but also encourages a connection to the natural world.

What Your Child Learns from This:

• Imagination and Creativity: This activity nurtures creative thinking as your child uses cotton balls and other materials to recreate the ever-changing shapes of clouds.

• Weather Exploration: It introduces basic weather concepts, such as cloud types, shapes, and how clouds form.

• Fine Motor Skills: By gluing, shaping, and arranging cotton balls, your child will practice hand-eye coordination and dexterity.

• Artistic Expression: Your child will learn how to visually represent a natural phenomenon, connecting art and science.

Materials Needed (Consider listing options):

- Cotton balls (to form the clouds)
- Construction paper or cardboard (for the base)
- Glue (to hold the cotton balls in place)
- Markers or crayons (to add detail to the scene)
- Optional: Glitter (to make "sparkly clouds")
- Optional: Scissors (for cutting paper shapes)
- Optional: Cotton swabs (to create smaller clouds or add detail)

Step-by-Step Instructions:

1. Introduce the Cloud Concept

• *Parent's Prompt: "Did you know that clouds are made of tiny water droplets? Some clouds are fluffy, while others are dark and heavy. Today, we're going to create our own clouds!"*

• Discuss the types of clouds (e.g., cumulus, cirrus, stratus) and ask your child to describe what kind of cloud they would like to make.

2. Prepare the Base

• *Parent's Prompt: "Let's start by getting our base ready. We'll use the construction paper as the sky, but feel free to make it look however you like! What color would you like your sky to be? Maybe it's a sunny day or a cloudy afternoon?"*

• Set up the construction paper or cardboard, allowing your child to decide on a background (e.g., blue for a clear sky or grey for a stormy look).

3. Shape the Clouds

• *Parent's Prompt: "Now, let's make our clouds! Take a cotton ball and pull it apart to make it look like a fluffy cloud. What* shape do you think your cloud should be? Big and round, or long and wispy?"

• Encourage your child to pull apart cotton balls and glue them onto the paper. They can create large, puffy clouds or smaller wisps.

4. Add Details

• *Parent's Prompt: "Can we make our cloud look more real? You can add some extra details! How about drawing a sun peeking through the clouds or a rainbow next to your cloud?"*

• Use markers, crayons, or glitter to add finishing touches. Let your child add details like the sun, birds, or a rainbow, imagining the story of the cloud in the sky.

5. Cloud Sculpture Reflection

• *Parent's Prompt: "What does your cloud look like? Is it floating high in the sky, or does it look like a raincloud? Do you think it's going to rain or just float away?"*

• After finishing, ask your child to explain the cloud they've created. This sparks storytelling and further exploration of the natural world.

Reflective Questions to Deepen the Experience:

- *"What does your cloud feel like? Is it soft and fluffy or a bit heavy?"*
- *"What do you think your cloud is doing right now? Is it moving across the sky?"*
- *"How do you think the cloud would change if it started to rain?"*
- *"If we could jump into your cloud, what do you think it would be like?"*
- *"Do you think your cloud is happy or sad? Why?"*
- *"How could we make a rainbow come out of our cloud? What colors would it be?"*
- *"What shapes can you make with your clouds? Can you turn it into something else, like a lion or a boat?"*
- *"What happens when clouds get too full of water?"*
- *"What kind of weather do you think your cloud brings? Is it sunny or stormy?"*
- *"What if your cloud turns into a thunderstorm? What would happen to your sky?"*

Bonus Challenges or Variations:

• Cloud Type Challenge: Learn about different cloud types (e.g., cirrus, cumulus, stratus) and create different sculptures based on each type. Try making a big, puffy cumulus cloud, or a long, wispy cirrus cloud!

• Weather Storytelling: Once you've created several clouds, come up with a weather story together. Does one cloud bring a storm? Does another bring a sunny day?

• Moving Clouds: Take this activity outdoors! After making the cloud sculptures, head outside and look at the real clouds in the sky. Try to spot clouds that look like animals, faces, or other fun shapes.

• Cloud Texture Art: Try mixing cotton balls with other textured materials like yarn or fabric to create different textures for the clouds, adding depth and variation to your cloud sculptures.

Why This Activity Matters:

This activity provides a wonderful opportunity for children to express their creativity while learning about weather patterns and cloud formations. It combines art, science, and storytelling, fostering curiosity about the natural world and how we can recreate it through imagination and craft. By shaping and designing their own clouds, children get to connect with the world around them in a hands-on and meaningful way.

6. WILD ART SAFARI

Objective:

Embark on a wild, creative adventure where your child becomes a nature explorer and an artist. Together, you will create art inspired by animals, plants, and the natural world around you. This activity blends exploration with creativity, fostering an appreciation for wildlife and developing your child's artistic expression.

Activity Overview:

In this Wild Art Safari, you and your child will transform everyday materials into artistic representations of wild animals and plants. By observing real-life creatures or imaginative wildlife, your child will learn how to use colors, textures, and shapes to express their understanding of the natural world. Whether creating animal prints or painting landscapes, this activity fosters connection with nature while encouraging artistic exploration.

What Your Child Learns from This:

• Artistic Skills: Your child will practice using different artistic tools and techniques, such as painting, drawing, and texture creation, which helps develop fine motor skills.

• Nature Observation: By closely observing animals, plants, or even imaginary creatures, your child learns to see the beauty in the natural world and how to express that beauty creatively.

• Creative Problem-Solving: When deciding how to represent various animals or elements of nature, your child will exercise imagination and resourcefulness.

• Appreciation for Wildlife: This activity helps foster empathy and interest in the diversity of life on Earth, from jungle creatures to forest dwellers.

Materials Needed (Consider listing options):

• Art supplies: Crayons, markers, colored pencils, paints (watercolors, tempera), or pastels

• Paper (various types for different textures)

• Stamps or animal figurines (to create animal prints)

• Nature objects: Leaves, twigs, pinecones, pebbles (for texture)

• Glue or mod-podge

• Optional: Animal stickers, feathers, fabric scraps (for added texture)

Step-by-Step Instructions:

1. Set the Safari Scene

• *Parent's Prompt: "We're about to head on a Wild Art Safari! Are you ready to explore the world of animals and nature? Let's look at the creatures in the wild, and we'll create our own art inspired by them!"*

• Discuss animals you both love—whether it's jungle animals, birds, or sea creatures—and decide which one to start with. Explore nature books or online images to spark your child's imagination.

2. Animal Observation

• *Parent's Prompt: "Let's take a close look at this animal. How would you describe its colors? Its shape? What does it do in the wild?"*

• Spend a few minutes observing pictures or videos of wild animals, noticing key features like fur, feathers, scales, or patterns. If possible, visit a park or zoo for live inspiration.

3. Create the Art

• *Parent's Prompt: "Now, let's use colors, shapes, and textures to create your version of this animal. What materials will you use? Will your lion's mane be fluffy or spiky?"*

• Begin by drawing or painting the animal or plant, paying attention to the colors and textures. Encourage your child to experiment with different materials like markers, paint, and natural items like leaves to create interesting textures.

4. Add Texture and Detail

• *Parent's Prompt: "How can we make the fur of the tiger look soft? Should we add twigs to your art to create a jungle effect?"*

• Incorporate textured elements into your artwork. Use objects from nature (twigs, leaves, feathers) or materials like fabric and cotton to give the art a more tactile, layered feel.

5. Safari Reflection

• *Parent's Prompt: "What do you think this animal is feeling? What could it be doing in the wild right now?"*

• Once the artwork is complete, talk with your child about their piece. Ask them to describe their creation and what it represents. Encourage them to think about the animal's life in the wild and how it survives or thrives.

6. Gallery Time

• *Parent's Prompt: "Let's hang up your Wild Art Safari creations! You're an artist now!"*

• After completing the artwork, display it proudly in your home. Turn it into a mini-gallery for the whole family to enjoy!

Reflective Questions to Deepen the Experience:

- *"What do you think makes an elephant's ears so big? How can we make them look real in your artwork?"*
- *"What's the wildest animal you can imagine? What would it look like? What colors would it have?"*
- *"Why do you think a giraffe has such a long neck? What shapes or lines could you use to show its height?"*
- *"How would you show a lion's strength in your artwork? What colors can show its power?"*
- *"What does the texture of an animal's skin feel like? Could we use different materials to show that texture?"*
- *"If your animal could talk, what would it say? How can we show that in the art?"*
- *"What kind of environment does your animal live in? How can we show that in your artwork?"*
- *"What would happen if we combined two animals to make a new one? What would it look like?"*
- *"What part of your animal do you love the most? How can we make that stand out in your picture?"*
- *"Why do you think animals have different colors and textures? How can we make our art match nature?"*

Bonus Challenges or Variations:

• Nature Printmaking: Use leaves, animal figurines, or stamps to create prints on paper. This helps explore textures and patterns found in nature.

• Animal Collage: Instead of drawing, create a collage using magazines, fabric scraps, or nature items to build an animal scene.

• Safari Adventure Book: Turn your child's art into a storybook. Each page can feature a different animal they've created, and together you can make up an adventure for each.

• Eco-Friendly Safari: Use only recycled materials to create your art, learning about sustainability while making your masterpiece.

Why This Activity Matters:

This activity encourages both artistic expression and a love for the natural world. Your child will enjoy the process of creating while deepening their understanding of animals and their environments. It also gives them a chance to experiment with different art forms, boosting creativity and fine motor skills.

7. TIME TRAVELER'S TOOLKIT

Objective:

Embark on a journey through time with your child using a DIY "Time Traveler's Toolkit." This imaginative and hands-on activity fosters an understanding of history, problem-solving, and creativity, while exploring the idea of time travel. Your child will design their own time machine, create tools for their travels, and role-play as explorers of different eras in history.

Activity Overview:

In this activity, you and your child will craft a "Time Traveler's Toolkit" complete with magical tools for their journey through time. Each piece of the toolkit represents a different time period, helping your child explore and imagine themselves in ancient civilizations, future worlds, and everything in between. From ancient Egyptian scrolls to futuristic gadgets, they'll create, problem-solve, and use their imagination to travel through time and learn about different periods of history.

What Your Child Learns from This:

• Historical Exploration: Your child will learn about different time periods and cultures, sparking curiosity about history.

• Creative Problem Solving: Designing their own time-traveling tools will encourage imaginative thinking and hands-on creativity.

• Imaginative Play: Role-playing as time travelers allows your child to think about the world in new and exciting ways.

• Storytelling and Writing: As they create their toolkit, they'll also engage in storytelling, imagining where and when they will travel and why.

Materials Needed (Consider listing options):

• Cardboard boxes or tubes (for creating the "time machine" or tool handles)

• Markers, paint, and stickers (for decorating the tools)

• Aluminum foil (for futuristic gadgets or time machine parts)

• String or yarn (to tie "mystical" artifacts or tools together)

• Paper and scissors (for making maps, scrolls, or instructions)

• Empty bottles or small jars (to hold "time crystals" or potions)

• Stamps, old coins, or decorative paper (for historical time-travel items)

• Glue or tape (for assembling the pieces of the toolkit)

Step-by-Step Instructions:

1. Create Your Time Machine

• *Parent's Prompt: "Let's start by building the most important thing for your time travels–a time machine! What does it look like? Is it a shiny spaceship or an ancient Egyptian chariot?"*

• Use cardboard to create a simple "time machine." Let your child decorate it with markers, paint, or even aluminum foil for a futuristic feel. You can use a cardboard box as a "control center" or make a wearable time-travel vest!

2. Design the Tools

• *Parent's Prompt: "Every time traveler needs special tools! What do you think you'll need? Maybe a compass to find your way or a special key to unlock time?"*

• Use the materials at hand to create tools like a compass, map, "time crystals" in bottles, or even a "time travel watch." Encourage your child to think about what kind of items they might need to travel through different time periods–whether it's a magic scroll for medieval times or a gadget for space adventures.

3. Prepare for a Time Travel Adventure

• *Parent's Prompt: "Now that you have your toolkit, where will you go? Are you traveling to the future to meet robots or to ancient Egypt to discover pyramids?"*

• Have your child plan a journey. Will they go to the dinosaurs, the space age, or the past to meet kings and queens? Help them create a map or journal of where they might travel next.

4. Time Travel Role Play

• *Parent's Prompt: "Alright, let's get into character! We've just landed in ancient Greece—how are we going to talk to the people there? What tools do we need?"*

• Once the tools and time machine are ready, let your child role-play as a time traveler. Use the tools they created and explore different time periods together. They can visit any era —use your imagination to invent characters, adventures, and tasks that fit the time period.

5. Storytelling

• *Parent's Prompt: "What happens when you go back in time? Do you help someone? Do you have to solve a mystery?"*

• Encourage your child to tell a story about their time travel. They can write a short story or share verbally what happens when they use their toolkit to navigate time. You can even make it into an ongoing story, where every day they "travel" to a new place and add to their adventures.

Reflective Questions to Deepen the Experience:

- *"Which time period do you want to visit next? Why?"*
- *"What do you think people in ancient times used to travel? How do you think their tools were different from ours?"*
- *"What problem would you want to solve as a time traveler? Who could you help?"*
- *"What did you find most interesting about the time periods we explored today?"*
- *"Do you think time travel could really happen? What kind of machine would you want to use?"*
- *"What do you think you could learn from meeting people in the future?"*
- *"How would your tools change if you were visiting the future? What new gadgets would you need?"*
- *"If you could time travel for real, where would you go and what would you do there?"*
- *"What do you think people in the past might have imagined about time travel?"*
- *"What other tools could we make for our toolkit to help us on our next adventure?"*

Bonus Challenges or Variations:

• Historical Timeline Adventure: Choose a specific time period, like ancient Egypt or the Wild West, and learn a bit about it before your time travel adventure. Create artifacts, costumes, or even simple activities based on the time period you're exploring.

• Future Time Traveler's Gadgets: Imagine a future world—what tools or gadgets would you need to survive in space, underwater, or on a different planet? Let your child design futuristic gadgets!

• Time Travel Diaries: Keep a journal of your time travels. After each "adventure," have your child write (or dictate) what happened, where they went, and what they learned. You could even make a scrapbook of their travels!

Why This Activity Matters:

Through the Time Traveler's Toolkit, your child will embark on exciting, imaginative journeys while learning about history, science, and storytelling. This activity combines creativity with learning, allowing for endless possibilities and exploration of the world around us—past, present, and future!

8. MONSTER MASH-UP

Objective:

Encourage your child's creativity and motor skills by designing a one-of-a-kind monster using various craft supplies, all while exploring different textures, colors, and shapes.

Activity Overview:

In this fun and hands-on craft activity, your child will use their imagination to create their own monster from scratch. With a variety of materials to choose from, they'll combine different textures, colors, and features to design a unique creature. This activity also promotes fine motor skills, hand-eye coordination, and gives a great opportunity for storytelling as your child creates the monster's backstory and personality.

What Your Child Learns from This:

• Creativity and Imagination: Your child will use their imagination to invent a monster, deciding on its look, personality, and story.

• Fine Motor Skills: As your child glues, cuts, and arranges pieces, they'll improve their hand-eye coordination and dexterity.

• Color and Shape Recognition: This activity allows your child to explore colors, shapes, and patterns, helping to enhance their visual-spatial skills.

• Storytelling: Once the monster is made, your child will have the chance to create a story around their creation, fostering both verbal and narrative skills.

• Decision-Making: They'll make choices about which materials work best together to create their monster, boosting their problem-solving abilities.

Materials Needed (Consider listing options):

• Colored paper or craft foam (for monster body and limbs)

• Googly eyes (for extra fun!)

• Pipe cleaners (to create hair, arms, or legs)

• Pom-poms (to add texture or a "fuzzy" feel)

• Fabric scraps or felt (for monster clothes, wings, or additional features)

• Markers or crayons (for decorating and adding details)

• Scissors (for cutting shapes and materials)

• Glue, tape, or a glue gun (to stick everything together)

• Optional: Glitter, stickers, or sequins (for extra sparkle and embellishments)

• Optional: Craft sticks (to add structure for arms or legs)

Step-by-Step Instructions:

1. Set the Stage for Monster Creation

• *Parent's Prompt: "Let's create a monster, but what kind of monster will it be? A silly monster, a spooky one, or something entirely new?"*

• Start by brainstorming with your child about what kind of monster they'd like to make. You can ask fun questions like, "Does your monster have fur or scales?" or "Does it have three eyes or six?"

2. Choose the Monster's Body and Features

• *Parent's Prompt: "What shape should the body be? A round monster, a square one, or maybe one with tentacles?"*

• Let your child cut out the body parts from paper, foam, or fabric. Use different shapes and textures to create the body, arms, legs, or even wings. Encourage them to think about the monster's mood–do they want it to look friendly or a little bit mischievous?

3. Add Details for Personality

• *Parent's Prompt: "Now let's add some eyes and a mouth. Should it have a big, scary grin or a tiny smile? How about teeth?"*

• Use googly eyes, buttons, or paper to create eyes, and let your child add a mouth. Don't forget to add any other features like ears, horns, or noses to give the monster character.

4. Decorate and Embellish

• *Parent's Prompt: "Let's make your monster even cooler with some extra details. How about some glitter for sparkles or some pom-poms for a fluffy monster?"*

• Let your child add any extra accessories like glitter, feathers, or stickers. They can make the monster look even more unique with fun textures or special features.

5. Create a Monster Backstory

• *Parent's Prompt: "What's your monster's name? What kind of adventures does it go on? Does it live in a magical forest, or does it love to explore space?"*

• Once the monster is finished, ask your child to tell a story about it. Who is the monster friends with? What's its favorite thing to do? This part helps your child develop their storytelling skills.

Reflective Questions to Deepen the Experience:

- *"What does your monster look like? What kind of personality does it have?"*
- *"How does your monster feel today? Happy, angry, or silly?"*
- *"What is your monster's favorite food? Does it like pizza or prefer something spooky like worms?"*
- *"Where does your monster live? In a forest, a cave, or under the bed?"*
- *"What would happen if your monster met another one? Would they be friends or have a funny fight?"*
- *"Can your monster talk? What kind of voice does it have?"*
- *"What would your monster do if it had a superpower?"*
- *"How would you feel if you met your monster in real life?"*
- *"What kind of creature would be the monster's best friend?"*
- *"If your monster could be any color, what would it be? What about its favorite color?"*

Bonus Challenges or Variations:

• Monster Family: Encourage your child to create an entire monster family–mom, dad, and little monsters. Each one can have a different feature (e.g., big teeth, big feet, or lots of fur).

• Monster Movement: After creating the monster, create a monster dance! Have your child make the monster move in funny ways–wiggling, hopping, or even rolling!

• Monster Printables: Use printable monster faces that children can cut out and decorate with different materials for a quicker, simpler version.

• Interactive Story: Turn the monster's adventures into a puppet show. After creating your monster, use it to act out a short story where the monster goes on an adventure or solves a problem.

Why This Activity Matters:

This activity is not only fun and creative, but it also helps to develop your child's motor skills, creativity, and storytelling abilities. By the end of the craft, your child will have created a one-of-a-kind monster that has its own special story to tell!

9. DIY STORY DICE

Objective:

Create a fun and engaging activity that sparks your child's creativity, storytelling skills, and imagination through a simple DIY craft. The story dice will give your child endless combinations of story prompts, helping them create unique tales every time!

Activity Overview:

Story dice are a fantastic tool to boost creativity and problem-solving skills. With just a few simple materials, you and your child can create a set of dice that inspire endless stories. This activity encourages children to think outside the box, combine random elements, and practice narrative skills. By rolling the dice, your child will be able to create unique, fun, and often wacky stories—perfect for language development and imaginative play.

What Your Child Learns from This:

• Storytelling and Language Skills: By creating and telling their own stories, your child will improve their language skills, vocabulary, and narrative structure.

• Creativity and Imagination: This activity pushes children to come up with new ideas based on the dice rolls, stimulating their creativity.

• Problem Solving: When the dice provide random prompts, your child will need to think critically to connect the ideas and make sense of the story.

• Fine Motor Skills: Crafting the dice and rolling them helps improve fine motor skills and hand-eye coordination.

Materials Needed (Consider listing options):

• 6 empty dice (wooden, foam, or cardboard)

• Markers or stickers (for drawing or writing story prompts on the dice)

• Paper and scissors (for making additional story elements if needed)

• Tape or glue (for securing stickers or paper to dice)

• Optional: Colored paper, washi tape, or decorative elements to make the dice visually appealing

Step-by-Step Instructions:

1. Prepare Your Dice

• *Parent's Prompt: "Let's make some magical story dice that will help us tell the best stories ever! Do you think our stories will involve dragons, treasure, or pirates?"*

• If you're using foam or wooden dice, simply set them aside. If using cardboard, you can make dice by cutting and folding paper to create a cube-like shape.

2. Decorate Your Dice with Story Prompts

• *Parent's Prompt: "What should we add to our dice? Maybe a picture of a dragon, a castle, or even a pirate ship? Let's make sure we have different ideas on each side!"*

• On each side of the dice, write or draw a different story prompt (e.g., characters like "pirate," "robot," "princess"), settings like "in the jungle" or "underwater," or objects like "treasure chest" or "magic potion." Be sure to mix nouns, verbs, and adjectives to make the dice as versatile as possible!

3. Get Ready to Play!

• *Parent's Prompt: "Let's get rolling! After we roll the dice, we'll use what comes up to tell a story. Are you ready to start? Let's see what we get!"*

• Roll the dice one by one, and use the prompts that land face-up to start telling a story. Combine the elements from each dice roll into a tale. You could say: "Once upon a time, a pirate (character) set sail to find a hidden treasure chest (object) deep in the jungle (setting)."

4. Create Your Story

• *Parent's Prompt: "Can we make the story more interesting by adding details? What if the treasure chest was cursed, or the pirate had a secret map?"*

• Let your child lead the story, using the dice prompts to guide their narrative. Encourage them to add twists and surprises, like an unexpected hero or a villain who changes the course of the adventure.

5. Reflect on the Story

• *Parent's Prompt: "What would happen if the pirate found the treasure? Do you think they'd share it, or would something go wrong?"*

• After completing the story, take a moment to discuss the events. Ask your child questions to help them think about the plot, characters, and setting in deeper ways. You can also challenge them to tell the story from another character's point of view or to change the ending.

Reflective Questions to Deepen the Experience:

- *"What happens if we change the character to a robot? How would the story change?"*
- *"If you could add one more dice, what would it show? A flying unicorn? A magic spell?"*
- *"What do you think happens after the story ends? Can you imagine what happens next?"*
- *"Would you want to be the hero in this story, or would you prefer to be the villain?"*
- *"How would the story change if the pirate didn't want the treasure? What would they do instead?"*
- *"What would you do if you were the dragon in the story?"*
- *"Can you think of a different ending where everything turns out differently?"*
- *"What if the main character could talk to animals? How would that change the adventure?"*
- *"If the setting of the story was a magical forest instead of a castle, how would that affect the story?"*
- *"What would happen if the hero and villain teamed up? What kind of story could they create together?"*

Bonus Challenges or Variations:

• Story Dice Challenge: Set a timer for 5 minutes and challenge your child to come up with the craziest story they can, using the dice rolls. The fun is in the rush to create something wild!

• Theme Your Dice: Make themed story dice, such as a fairy tale dice, superhero dice, or even a space adventure dice. Tailor the prompts to your child's interests.

• Story Dice for Group Play: If you have more children, they can each roll their own dice and take turns adding to a group story based on their dice prompts.

• Add Music or Sound Effects: As you tell the story, encourage your child to use music or sound effects to bring the tale to life. They can act out scenes or make sounds that match the characters and events.

Why This Activity Matters:

DIY Story Dice is a wonderful way for children to develop language skills, creativity, and storytelling techniques–all while having fun. It's also a great bonding activity where you, as a parent, can help spark new ideas and challenges for your child. Whether you use it as a daily creative exercise or as a special game for family time, these dice will be an endless source of fun stories!

10. SOUNDTRACK ADVENTURE

Objective:

To engage children in a sensory journey through sound and music, fostering creativity, emotional expression, and motor skills development. This activity encourages children to connect music with movement, helping them develop a greater understanding of rhythm, storytelling, and self-expression.

Activity Overview:

In this activity, your child will embark on an adventure where they get to create their own soundtrack to an imaginary story. They will explore various sounds, rhythms, and melodies, using instruments, body percussion, and their environment. Through this experience, they'll learn how music can influence emotions and actions, and how to connect sounds to specific scenarios.

What Your Child Learns from This:

• Music and Emotion Connection: Children will learn how different sounds and rhythms can make them feel different emotions–excited, calm, scared, or happy.

• Rhythm and Coordination: Using instruments or body percussion, children will practice rhythm and coordination, improving their fine and gross motor skills.

• Imagination and Storytelling: By creating their own soundtrack, children will stretch their imagination, as they connect music with movement and storytelling.

• Focus and Listening Skills: Children will enhance their ability to listen closely to music and use their focus to match the beat or rhythm in their movements.

Materials Needed (Consider listing options):

• Musical instruments (shakers, drums, tambourines, or even kitchen utensils like wooden spoons)

• Body percussion tools (hands, feet, clapping, or stomping)

• Music playlist with a variety of genres (classical, upbeat, slow, dramatic)

• Space to move around (clear the area to allow for dancing and movement)

• Optional: Sound-making toys like wind chimes, bells, or whistles to enhance the sound adventure.

Step-by-Step Instructions:

1. Set the Scene for the Adventure

• *Parent's Prompt: "We're going on an adventure today, and every part of our journey will have a different soundtrack. Let's start by imagining where we're going. Are we going to a jungle, a castle, or maybe exploring the deep ocean?"*

• Ask your child to think about the adventure, where it takes place, and what sounds they might hear on this adventure (birds chirping, waves crashing, or even a dragon's roar!).

2. Choose Your Instruments

• *Parent's Prompt: "What instruments will we need for our adventure? Let's pick up our shakers, or maybe the drum will be perfect for our journey through the forest!"*

• Let your child explore various instruments or create their own sounds using everyday objects. Encourage them to think about how the sound relates to the adventure you're imagining.

3. Create the Soundtrack

• *Parent's Prompt: "Now, let's make a sound for each part of our journey. Can we use the drum to make the sound of footsteps? How about some soft music to represent a calm forest or a wild sound for a thunderstorm?"*

• Play different songs or create your own rhythm to match different parts of the imaginary adventure. Encourage your child to dance or move to the rhythm. Discuss how the music makes them feel and what parts of the story the sound represents.

4. Move to the Beat

• *Parent's Prompt: "Let's dance and move along with the soundtrack! What happens when we play the music loudly? Does that change how we move? What about slow, soft sounds? How do you feel when we move slowly?"*

• Encourage your child to act out the adventure through movement, using the rhythm of the music to guide their actions. Slow, calming music might inspire them to move gently, while fast, upbeat music might encourage jumping and quick movements.

5. Reflection and Sharing

• *Parent's Prompt: "What part of the adventure did you like the most? Which sound made you feel the most excited or peaceful?"*

• After the soundtrack adventure, discuss the different sounds and movements. Ask your child what they enjoyed most and what sounds were their favorites.

Reflective Questions to Deepen the Experience:

- *"How did the music make you feel when we played it fast versus slow?"*
- *"If you were to tell the story again, what different sounds could you use to make it even more exciting?"*
- *"How do you think the music can help tell the story of our adventure?"*
- *"Which sound made you feel like you were on a grand adventure? Why?"*
- *"What was your favorite part of our journey, and what kind of music would go with it?"*
- *"How do you think our adventure would sound if we were in a desert? What kind of instruments would we need?"*
- *"If we were in a jungle, what sound would the trees make? What instruments could we use to make that sound?"*
- *"Can you make a sound that would represent a magic spell or a secret door opening?"*
- *"How did the beat of the music help you move your body? Did it make you feel faster or slower?"*
- *"If we went to space, what kind of music would we hear? What instruments could we use to make it sound like we were floating?"*

Bonus Challenges or Variations:

• Soundtrack Creation Challenge: Pick a movie or favorite show and recreate the soundtrack using only household items. Challenge your child to make their own version of the theme music or use sounds that match specific scenes.

• Nature Sounds: Take the soundtrack adventure outside! Explore sounds from nature (wind, birds, water) and create a musical story inspired by the environment.

• Musical Emotion Exploration: Play a variety of music that evokes different emotions and have your child act out how they feel with movement. Can they jump for excitement, spin for happiness, or move slowly for calmness?

• Storytelling with Sounds: After completing the soundtrack, try to tell a simple story using only sounds, no words. Ask your child to listen and guess what part of the story each sound represents.

Why This Activity Matters:

This activity is a fun and creative way for children to explore music, emotion, and movement while fostering imagination and expression. By connecting sound to storytelling, children learn to engage more deeply with both music and the world around them.

2. Cognitive Development and Memory

Cognitive development and memory are critical building blocks of a child's ability to learn, solve problems, and interact with the world. This chapter focuses on activities designed to stimulate critical thinking, enhance memory skills, and foster intellectual curiosity. By engaging in these exercises, children can develop stronger neural connections, improve recall, and build the problem-solving abilities needed for academic success and real-life situations. These activities also provide caregivers with opportunities to model curiosity and a love of learning, further enhancing their child's cognitive growth.

"Thinking: the talking of the soul with itself." - Plato

1. MEMORY MATCH MADNESS

Objective:

Memory Match Madness is a fast-paced game that boosts your child's memory, attention to detail, and cognitive flexibility. By flipping cards and matching pairs, your child will sharpen their short-term memory and learn to pay close attention to visual cues, all while having fun and working on their focus!

Activity Overview:

This game transforms the classic memory matching card game into a dynamic, interactive challenge. Through matching pairs of cards, your child will exercise their ability to recognize patterns, recall information, and practice patience. This simple but exciting game is great for fostering memory retention and concentration in young children.

What Your Child Learns from This:

• Memory Skills: Your child will improve their short-term memory by remembering where cards are placed and identifying matching pairs.

• Attention to Detail: The game helps children focus on small details and recognize patterns.

• Patience & Persistence: As the game involves turns and a waiting process, children learn the value of patience while continuing to try.

• Cognitive Flexibility: Memory Match Madness encourages children to quickly adapt their strategies and recall information from previous rounds.

• Social Skills: If played with others, the game promotes turn-taking, communication, and healthy competition.

Materials Needed (Consider listing options):

• Memory cards: You can use any set of cards with matching images, or make your own by using index cards or cardboard cut into squares.

• Stickers or drawings: You can draw matching pictures, animals, letters, numbers, or shapes on the cards.

• Timer (optional): To add a sense of urgency, you can set a timer to see how fast they can match pairs.

Step-by-Step Instructions:

1. Prepare the Cards:

• *Parent's Prompt: "Let's get our memory cards ready! We have pictures of animals, letters, or shapes, all mixed up."*

• Create pairs of matching cards, ensuring there is an even number. Shuffle them and spread them out face-down on a flat surface.

2. Explain the Rules:

• *Parent's Prompt: "Our goal is to find matching pairs of cards. We'll take turns flipping over two cards at a time. If they match, we get to keep them. If not, we turn them back over and try again!"*

• Let your child know they can only flip two cards per turn and that they'll need to remember where the others are.

3. Start the Game:

• *Parent's Prompt: "Ready to play? Let's flip over the first two cards!"*

• Take turns flipping two cards at a time. If the cards match, keep them; if not, turn them back over and let the next player take a turn.

4. Encourage Focus and Memory:

• *Parent's Prompt: "Do you remember where the last card was? Try to focus, you might find a match!"*

• Encourage your child to remember where specific cards are located to find matching pairs. The more they play, the better their memory skills will become.

5. End of the Game:

• *Parent's Prompt: "Great job! You found so many pairs! Let's count how many you matched. Would you like to play again?"*

• The game ends when all pairs have been matched. Count how many pairs each player matched, and celebrate their success.

Reflective Questions to Deepen the Experience:

• *"What made you remember where the cards were?"*

• *"Was there a specific strategy that helped you match the cards faster?"*

• *"Which pair was the hardest to remember? Why?"*

• *"How did you feel when you found a matching pair?"*

• *"Do you think you could play the game without turning the cards back over? How would that change the game?"*

• *"What did you do when you couldn't remember where the cards were? Did you try a different approach?"*

• *"What did you learn from playing with someone else?"*

• *"Can you think of a way to make this game harder?"*

• *"How do you think this game helps you remember things better in real life?"*

• *"If we had different pictures on the cards, how would that change the game?"*

Bonus Challenges or Variations:

• Timed Memory Challenge: Set a timer and see how many matches your child can make within a set time limit.

• Memory Match with Words: Use flashcards with simple words or letters and let your child match the words instead of pictures.

• Memory Match with Sounds: Instead of visual images, play matching sounds for your child to remember and match, like animal noises or instrument sounds.

• Team Play: If playing with multiple children, create teams where each team works together to find matching pairs. This promotes teamwork and collaboration.

• Memory Match with Categories: Use a set of cards that match by categories like animals, food, or colors, and have your child sort the cards accordingly.

Why This Activity Matters:

Memory Match Madness is a fun, engaging activity that enhances cognitive development, memory retention, and attention skills, all while keeping children entertained. With its competitive yet educational nature, this game is a perfect way for children to improve their cognitive skills and create lasting memories with family or friends!

2. PUZZLE PLAYTIME

Objective:

In this engaging and thoughtful activity, children will develop their cognitive and problem-solving abilities while having fun piecing together puzzles. Puzzle Playtime encourages critical thinking, spatial awareness, and patience as your child works through challenges in a playful and rewarding environment.

Activity Overview:

Puzzle Playtime is an opportunity for children to dive into the world of puzzles, from jigsaw to shape recognition. With each puzzle, children will sharpen their spatial skills, hand-eye coordination, and persistence as they work towards the final image or solution. This activity also promotes the development of memory, pattern recognition, and sequencing, all while boosting your child's confidence as they complete each puzzle.

What Your Child Learns from This:

• Problem-Solving Skills: By putting together pieces and finding the right fit, children learn how to approach and solve problems systematically.

• Spatial Awareness: Puzzles help children understand how different shapes fit together and how to visualize and manipulate objects in their mind.

• Focus and Patience: Completing a puzzle requires sustained concentration, teaching children the importance of patience and persistence.

• Memory: As they work through puzzles, children improve their memory by remembering where pieces go and recalling patterns or images.

• Fine Motor Skills: Handling small puzzle pieces boosts hand-eye coordination and fine motor control.

Materials Needed (Consider listing options):

• Jigsaw puzzles (Start with simple ones and gradually increase complexity)

• Shape sorters (For younger children, shape puzzles work well for basic classification and fine motor skills)

• Printable puzzles (Online printables or printable activity books for variety)

• Optional: For a twist, create custom puzzles using family photos, illustrations, or even homemade designs.

Step-by-Step Instructions:

1. Choose the Puzzle:

• *Parent's Prompt: "Let's start with a fun puzzle! We've got one with animals, or we can try the one with the big blue ocean. Which one would you like to do first?"*

• Select a puzzle appropriate for your child's age and difficulty level. If they are beginners, start with a smaller puzzle with fewer pieces.

2. Unveil the Pieces:

• *Parent's Prompt: "Alright, let's see what pieces we have here! Can you find the corners and edges first?"*

• Lay out the puzzle pieces on a flat surface. Show your child how to identify the corner and edge pieces to help them build the framework of the puzzle.

3. Start Building the Border:

• *Parent's Prompt: "Let's start by making the edges. Can you find all the pieces that go on the outside? We'll build the frame first!"*

• Encourage your child to focus on assembling the edges of the puzzle, a helpful first step in any jigsaw puzzle.

4. Fill in the Middle:

• *Parent's Prompt: "Now let's work on the inside! Can you find the piece with the red car on it? I bet it's near the middle!"*

• Once the border is in place, begin filling in the middle sections. Guide your child by identifying images or patterns to help them find where each piece fits.

5. Problem-Solving and Trial and Error:

• *Parent's Prompt: "Hmm, this piece doesn't seem to fit. Let's try a different spot. What do you think?"*

• Encourage your child to think through trial and error and figure out where pieces might fit best. If they're stuck, offer hints without taking over, giving them the opportunity to solve problems independently.

6. Complete the Puzzle:

• *Parent's Prompt: "We're almost there! Just a couple more pieces. Can you find where they go?"*

• Celebrate the accomplishment once the puzzle is complete, and encourage your child to step back and admire the finished work.

7. Reflect on the Puzzle Experience:

• *Parent's Prompt: "You did such a great job! What part of the puzzle was the hardest for you? What was the most fun part?"*

• After completing the puzzle, ask reflective questions to deepen the learning experience.

Reflective Questions to Deepen the Experience:

- *"What did you learn about how the pieces fit together?"*
- *"Can you remember the first piece you placed? How did you know where it went?"*
- *"What strategy helped you when you couldn't find a piece?"*
- *"Do you think the picture looks different now that it's complete? What do you notice?"*
- *"Was there a piece that was really hard to place? How did you figure it out?"*
- *"What do you think would happen if we tried a bigger puzzle?"*
- *"What shapes do you see in the puzzle? Can you find other things around the house that have these shapes?"*
- *"How do you feel now that the puzzle is finished?"*
- *"What was your favorite part of the puzzle? Was it the beginning, middle, or end?"*
- *"How did working together help us finish the puzzle faster?"*

Bonus Challenges or Variations:

• Time Challenge: Race against the clock to complete the puzzle as quickly as possible! How much faster can you do it next time?

• Puzzle Mix-Up: Once your child gets the hang of the puzzle, try mixing pieces from two puzzles together to increase the challenge.

• Create Your Own Puzzle: Draw or print a simple picture and cut it into puzzle pieces for a homemade challenge.

• Memory Challenge: Try doing the puzzle without looking at the image. Can your child remember what the finished puzzle looks like and put it together based on memory alone?

Why This Activity Matters:

Puzzle Playtime is an excellent activity for developing critical thinking skills while keeping children engaged in a fun and active way. It encourages patience, attention to detail, and problem-solving, all while fostering a sense of accomplishment as they complete the puzzle. Whether your child is just starting with simple puzzles or tackling more complex ones, Puzzle Playtime will help them build essential skills that will benefit them in many areas of life.

3. COLORFUL COUNTING ADVENTURE

Objective:

The Colorful Counting Adventure turns counting into an imaginative and colorful journey! Children will count objects while exploring their colors and patterns, strengthening their numerical skills while also developing an understanding of shapes, colors, and sorting. This activity is a playful and creative way to practice early math concepts.

Activity Overview:

In this adventure, your child will not only count but also categorize objects by color, creating a vibrant, hands-on learning experience. The Colorful Counting Adventure takes counting beyond numbers and integrates it with visual learning, making it a multisensory experience. Whether it's sorting colorful beads, arranging colored blocks, or collecting objects from around the house, this activity encourages children to see numbers in new and exciting ways.

What Your Child Learns from This:

• Counting Skills: Your child will practice counting up to 20 (or higher), which builds early numeracy skills.

• Color Recognition: As your child sorts and organizes by color, they reinforce their ability to identify and differentiate colors.

• Categorization: Learning to group objects by color helps with early classification skills, an important aspect of cognitive development.

• Fine Motor Skills: Handling small objects like beads or blocks helps strengthen hand-eye coordination and dexterity.

• Spatial Awareness: Arranging objects in different patterns and sequences improves a child's spatial reasoning.

Materials Needed (Consider listing options):

• A variety of colored objects (blocks, beads, buttons, crayons, or even colored paper)

• Sorting trays or containers (optional but helpful for organizing different colors)

• Markers or stickers to label different color categories

• Timer (optional, to add a challenge)

• Optional: Colored paper, colored foam shapes, or fabric swatches for added texture

Step-by-Step Instructions:

1. Prepare the Colorful Objects:

• *Parent's Prompt: "Let's go on a Colorful Counting Adventure! We need to find objects around the house that are all different colors. Can you find something red, blue, and yellow?"*

• Gather a variety of objects in different colors. It can be anything from toys to clothing items, craft supplies, or kitchen utensils!

2. Set Up the Sorting Areas:

• *Parent's Prompt: "Now that we've got our colorful objects, let's sort them into different piles. Can you place all the red things in this pile, and all the blue things in this pile?"*

• Label the sorting areas or containers with color names, and encourage your child to match the objects accordingly.

3. Count and Group:

• *Parent's Prompt: "Okay, let's count how many blue objects we have. How many are there? One, two, three...keep going!"*

• Help your child count the objects in each category. For younger children, start with small numbers and gradually increase as they master counting.

4. Create Colorful Patterns:

• *Parent's Prompt: "Can we create a pattern with these colored items? Let's try red, blue, red, blue. What comes next?"*

• Challenge your child to arrange the items in simple color patterns. You can start with AB patterns and increase complexity as they progress.

5. Race the Clock (Optional):

• *Parent's Prompt: "Let's see if we can do it faster this time! How many blue items can we find in one minute?"*

• Add a sense of excitement by timing how quickly your child can sort and count each color. This adds an element of friendly competition.

6. Reflect on the Adventure:

• *Parent's Prompt: "You did an amazing job! How many colors did we use today? Which was your favorite to count? What other objects can we sort by color around the house?"*

• Ask your child to reflect on what they learned and what their favorite part of the adventure was.

Reflective Questions to Deepen the Experience:

- *"How many red objects did you find? Can you count them again to double-check?"*
- *"What color was the hardest to find? Why do you think that is?"*
- *"What's your favorite color, and why? Can we find that color in different objects?"*
- *"How do the patterns look when we mix the colors up? Can we make a new pattern?"*
- *"Can you think of another way to sort the objects? By size? Shape?"*
- *"If we counted more objects, do you think we would need more or fewer colors?"*
- *"What happens if we change the pattern? Can you make a pattern of three colors?"*
- *"What do you think is the most important thing when sorting? What helps you decide where things go?"*
- *"How many colors are in a rainbow? Can we find those colors today?"*
- *"If we keep sorting like this every day, how fast do you think we can get at it?"*

Bonus Challenges or Variations:

• Speed Sorting Challenge: Race to see how many objects you can sort by color in 30 seconds.

• Color Mixing: For older children, explore color theory by mixing primary colors (red, blue, yellow) to see what new colors can be made.

• Creative Color Art: After sorting, encourage your child to use the sorted objects to create a colorful collage or artwork.

• Sorting by Size and Color: Add a level of complexity by sorting objects by both color and size (e.g., small blue objects, large red objects).

• Color Adventure Walk: Go on a walk around the house or outside to find objects in different colors, then sort them when you return.

Why This Activity Matters:

The Colorful Counting Adventure is a great way to turn everyday objects into a vibrant learning experience. It brings together counting, color recognition, sorting, and pattern making into an engaging and interactive adventure. This activity supports your child's early math skills while fostering creativity and hands-on learning in a playful, fun setting!

4. STORY SEQUENCING CHALLENGE

Objective:

In the Story Sequencing Challenge, children will build their narrative skills while practicing logic and memory. Through this activity, they will learn to organize events in a logical order, which helps improve their understanding of storytelling and enhances their cognitive development.

Activity Overview:

The Story Sequencing Challenge encourages children to arrange story cards or images in the correct order. As they do, they'll explore concepts of cause and effect, timing, and sequence. This hands-on activity also nurtures their creativity as they are invited to expand on the story and add their own twists. By sequencing events, children practice thinking in a linear fashion, helping them build foundational skills for reading comprehension, writing, and problem-solving.

What Your Child Learns from This:

• Storytelling: Children learn how to structure a story with a beginning, middle, and end.

• Critical Thinking: Sorting out the sequence of events requires logical thinking and understanding the relationships between different actions.

• Memory Skills: As they recall details from a story or scenario, children strengthen their memory and recall abilities.

• Creative Expression: Encourages children to think creatively and invent their own versions of stories.

• Cause and Effect: Children understand how one action leads to the next and how different events are connected.

Materials Needed (Consider listing options):

• Story cards or images (create your own with illustrations, or use picture books and cut out key scenes)

• Paper and pen for creating your own story templates

• Optional: Printable story sequencing worksheets

• Optional: A timer for added challenge

Step-by-Step Instructions:

1. Prepare the Story Cards:

• *Parent's Prompt: "Let's make our own story! We have pictures from our favorite book, or we can make new ones. We'll use these to build a fun story together."*

• Choose a simple story or create a set of cards with different scenes. These could be images from a book, a movie, or even scenarios you invent together.

2. Arrange the Story Cards:

• *Parent's Prompt: "Let's look at these pictures and try to figure out what happens first, second, and last. What do you think comes before this? And what happens after?"*

• Mix up the cards and ask your child to arrange them in the order they think makes sense. Help them understand the flow of the story and what happens first, next, and finally.

3. Tell the Story:

• *Parent's Prompt: "Now that the pictures are in order, let's tell the story! What do you think happens in the middle? How do we get from this part to the next?"*

• As your child places each card in order, help them expand on each scene by asking questions about what happens next and encouraging them to think about the details.

4. Discuss the Story Flow:

• *Parent's Prompt: "How do the different parts of the story connect? What happens if we change the order of the pictures?"*

• Once the story is arranged, discuss with your child why certain events need to happen in a specific order and how the sequence affects the outcome of the story.

5. Create a New Ending (Optional):

• *Parent's Prompt: "What if we change one part of the story? How could we end it differently?"*

• Encourage your child to get creative and alter parts of the story, imagining how different choices would change the plot. You could even add a twist to the original ending!

Reflective Questions to Deepen the Experience:

- *"What happens if we change the order of the cards? Does the story still make sense?"*
- *"Why do you think this event happens first? What would happen if we switched it with something else?"*
- *"How does the main character feel at the beginning versus the end? What changed?"*
- *"Can you think of a way to make the story longer? What would happen next?"*
- *"Why is it important to tell a story in a certain order?"*
- *"What's your favorite part of the story? Why?"*
- *"If you could change one part of the story, what would it be?"*
- *"Do you think a different order of events would make the story more exciting or sadder?"*
- *"If we added another character, what role would they play in the story?"*
- *"What do you think happens before or after the last event? Can you imagine what happens next?"*

Bonus Challenges or Variations:

• Timed Challenge: See how quickly your child can arrange the story cards in the correct order. You could also make it a race to see who can arrange their cards the fastest!

• Create Your Own Cards: Encourage your child to draw their own pictures or write out events, creating a story from scratch. This adds an extra creative element.

• Non-Verbal Sequencing: Instead of using pictures, use written words and have your child read the sentences to figure out the correct sequence.

• Interactive Storytelling: After sequencing, act out the story with your child, turning it into a performance. This will enhance both their language and social skills.

• Mixed-Up Story: Mix up multiple stories and ask your child to sort the scenes from several different narratives into their correct order.

Why This Activity Matters:

The Story Sequencing Challenge is an engaging and educational activity that fosters logical thinking, creativity, and storytelling skills in children. By sequencing stories and understanding how events unfold, kids learn to make sense of the world around them in a structured yet imaginative way. This challenge will spark their curiosity and ignite their love for narratives, encouraging them to explore and create stories of their own!

5. MEMORY OBSTACLE COURSE

Objective:

This fun and dynamic activity encourages children to improve both their memory and physical coordination. The Memory Obstacle Course combines physical movement with cognitive challenges, where children have to remember and retrieve information while navigating through an obstacle course. It's designed to enhance memory recall, focus, and motor planning skills–all while having a blast!

Activity Overview:

The Memory Obstacle Course is an exciting way to engage your child's mind and body. In this activity, children will move through a series of physical challenges, each with a corresponding memory task. Whether it's jumping over cushions or remembering patterns of objects, your child will have to use their memory and physical agility to succeed. This activity enhances both cognitive and physical skills, and the varying challenges keep it exciting and stimulating.

What Your Child Learns from This:

• Memory Enhancement: Strengthening memory recall by remembering the sequence of obstacles or specific instructions.

• Physical Coordination: Enhancing motor skills by moving through various obstacles such as hopping, crawling, or balancing.

• Focus and Concentration: Keeping focus while completing a series of tasks that require both mental and physical effort.

• Problem-Solving: Thinking through each challenge and figuring out the best way to tackle the memory and physical tasks.

Materials Needed (Consider listing options):

• Soft objects for obstacles (pillows, chairs, cushions, or cones)

• Markers or tape to create boundaries and markers

• Memory items (cards, small toys, or pictures)

• Timer or stopwatch

• A safe space for running and climbing (indoor or outdoor)

• Optional: Music for added energy and rhythm

Step-by-Step Instructions:

1. Set Up the Obstacle Course:

• *Parent's Prompt: "Let's build a course! We're going to set up a path where you have to jump, crawl, and balance, but here's the twist—you'll also have to remember things along the way!"*

• Create an obstacle course using pillows to jump over, chairs to crawl under, or cones to zigzag around. You can also place memory challenges at specific points (e.g., a pile of flashcards or objects that need to be remembered).

2. Create Memory Stations:

• *Parent's Prompt: "At each station, we'll put a memory challenge! For example, you might have to remember a color pattern, a sequence of objects, or where certain items are hidden."*

• At different points in the obstacle course, introduce a memory task. For instance, you could lay out five cards with different images on them and ask your child to memorize the order. After completing the obstacle, they'll need to recall what they saw.

3. Start the Course:

• *Parent's Prompt: "Ready, set, go! First, you'll jump over these pillows, then crawl under the chair, and when you reach the cards, you'll try to remember the order!"*

• As your child moves through the obstacles, encourage them to keep their focus on the memory task at each checkpoint.

4. Check the Memory Challenge:

• *Parent's Prompt: "You made it to the cards! Now, what's the order of the images you saw earlier? Can you remember them?"*

• After completing the obstacle, pause to see if your child can recall the memory challenge. Help them if necessary, but encourage them to think through it on their own.

5. Repeat the Course:

• *Parent's Prompt: "Let's try it again! Can you remember the images even better this time? Let's see if you can go faster, too!"*

• After completing the course once, have your child run it again. You can increase the complexity of the memory tasks or add more obstacles to keep things challenging.

6. Reflect on the Experience:

• *Parent's Prompt: "How did you do with the memory challenges? Was it harder when you had to run through the course and remember at the same time?"*

• After the activity, talk with your child about how they felt during the course and what strategies they used to remember things. Discuss how they can improve next time.

Reflective Questions to Deepen the Experience:

- *"What helped you remember the objects along the course?"*

- *"Which part of the course was the hardest to remember?"*

- *"Can you think of ways to make it easier to remember the tasks while moving through the obstacles?"*

- *"What would happen if we added more memory challenges to the course?"*

- *"How do you feel when you remember something after completing an obstacle?"*

- *"What other items could we use to create a memory challenge?"*

- *"Do you think your memory improved as you went through the course?"*

- *"Which obstacle did you enjoy the most? Why?"*

- *"How did you keep track of your memory tasks while running?"*

- *"Would you like to try making a memory course for me to run through?"*

Bonus Challenges or Variations:

• Timed Challenge: Add a timer to see how quickly your child can complete the obstacle course and still remember the memory tasks correctly.

• Memory Sequence: Increase the memory task difficulty by adding more items to remember in sequence (e.g., colors, numbers, or object locations).

• Obstacle Variety: Change the types of obstacles—use balance beams, tunnels, or jumping spots to add excitement.

• Team Memory Challenge: Partner up with your child for a team version, where each person is responsible for remembering part of the sequence.

Why This Activity Matters:

The Memory Obstacle Course not only keeps children physically active but also boosts their ability to focus, retain information, and solve problems. It's a fantastic way to combine fun and learning, offering valuable opportunities for your child to develop both mental and physical agility.

6. WHAT'S MISSING?

Objective:

In this activity, children practice observation, memory, and problem-solving by identifying what's missing from a collection of objects. This game promotes attentiveness, critical thinking, and memory retention, all while creating a fun and engaging challenge for young minds.

Activity Overview:

"What's Missing?" turns memory and observation into an exciting game. You'll present a set of objects to your child, briefly remove one or more, and challenge them to identify what's missing. This simple game can be adapted for different ages and abilities by adjusting the number of objects or the complexity of the items. It's an excellent way to nurture your child's memory and attention to detail, all while making it a playful experience that keeps them engaged.

What Your Child Learns from This:

• Memory Skills: By remembering which objects were present before they were taken away, children enhance their short-term memory.

• Observation Skills: This game encourages your child to notice details and make connections, boosting their visual and cognitive observation abilities.

• Problem-Solving: They learn how to think critically by identifying what's missing and using clues from the objects that remain.

• Focus and Attention: The challenge of remembering and identifying objects strengthens concentration and helps children practice patience.

Materials Needed (Consider listing options):

• A selection of small household items (blocks, toys, spoons, pencils, etc.)

• A small cloth or towel to cover objects (optional for added difficulty)

• Timer (optional, to time each round and make it more competitive)

• Optional: Items of different shapes, sizes, or colors for added variety and difficulty.

Step-by-Step Instructions:

1. Gather the Items:

• *Parent's Prompt: "Let's collect some things to play our game! We need a few toys or items that you can remember."*

• Choose 5-10 small objects from around the house. These can be toys, kitchen items, or everyday objects. Arrange them on a table or flat surface where your child can clearly see them.

2. Introduce the Game:

• *Parent's Prompt: "Here's how we're going to play–first, we'll look at all these items really carefully. I'll take something away, and then you'll have to guess what's missing!"*

• Encourage your child to closely examine the objects.

3. Hide an Object:

• *Parent's Prompt: "Now, I'm going to hide one object under this cloth. Ready? You'll need to use your memory to figure out which one is gone!"*

• Cover one or more items with a cloth or simply remove an object from the arrangement while your child isn't looking.

4. Guess What's Missing:

• *Parent's Prompt: "Can you guess what's missing? Take a good look and see if you can figure it out!"*

  • Ask your child to identify which object is missing. If they guess correctly, celebrate their success.

5. Increase Difficulty:

• *Parent's Prompt: "Great job! Now let's make it a little trickier. How about I hide two things at once?"*

  • For older children or those who get the hang of the game quickly, increase the challenge by hiding more objects or giving them less time to remember.

6. Reflect Together:

• *Parent's Prompt: "You did so well! What made it easier to remember the objects? Was there something about the way I arranged them that helped?"*

  • After each round, take a moment to talk about the process. Ask your child how they remembered the items and what helped them focus.

7. Repeat and Rethink:

• *Parent's Prompt: "Let's try again, but this time let's see if we can make the objects more tricky, like having items of the same color or shape."*

• Continue to play and adjust the difficulty based on your child's progress.

Reflective Questions to Deepen the Experience:

- *"How did you remember which items were on the table?"*

- *"What helped you notice what was missing?"*

- *"Do you think the game would be easier or harder if we used bigger items?"*

- *"How did you feel when you couldn't remember something at first? How did you figure it out?"*

- *"What can you do to make the game even harder? Maybe we can hide three things next time?"*

- *"How did the order of the objects help you remember them?"*

- *"Do you think you would remember things better if they were in a pattern or order?"*

- *"How would it feel if you had to guess without looking at the objects before they were hidden?"*

- *"Which part of the game was the most fun for you?"*

- *"Can we add a timer next time to see how fast we can remember?"*

Bonus Challenges or Variations:

• Speed Round: Use a timer to make each round faster, adding pressure and excitement. The challenge becomes not just memory, but speed too.

• Memory Matching: Add a matching element by pairing items together (e.g., a red ball and a blue block) and asking your child to remember the pairs.

• Pattern Play: Introduce patterns (e.g., red, blue, red, blue) with the objects and have your child guess what's missing from the sequence.

• Themed Missing: For older children, focus on thematic collections of objects (animals, shapes, etc.), helping them build categorization and memory.

• Story Time: Turn the game into a narrative by using small toys or figurines to create a short story. Afterward, ask what items were part of the story and which are missing.

Why This Activity Matters:

The "What's Missing?" game supports cognitive development by engaging your child's memory and attention. It's a simple yet effective way to help children develop their observational skills and problem-solving abilities, all while fostering confidence in their mental agility. Plus, the fun challenge of finding what's missing keeps them engaged and eager to play again! This activity helps lay the foundation for important learning skills that your child can build on in more complex tasks later on.

7. SHAPE AND SIZE SORTING

Objective:

Shape and Size Sorting is a foundational activity that helps children develop essential categorization, recognition, and problem-solving skills by sorting objects based on their shape and size. This activity is a fun way to teach children how to observe, identify, and classify, which supports their cognitive growth and fine motor skills.

Activity Overview:

This hands-on sorting activity challenges children to classify a variety of objects according to their shape (e.g., square, circle, triangle) and size (e.g., small, medium, large). Through this activity, children not only learn basic geometric concepts but also practice organizing objects in ways that enhance their understanding of the world around them. As they engage in sorting, they'll boost their focus, fine motor skills, and ability to make logical connections.

What Your Child Learns from This:

• Shape Recognition: Identifying different shapes helps children understand the world in a structured way, reinforcing early geometry concepts.

• Size Differentiation: Children learn to categorize objects by size, building their understanding of relative dimensions (big vs. small).

• Cognitive Development: Sorting and categorizing objects encourages logical thinking and memory recall as children recognize patterns.

• Fine Motor Skills: Picking up and placing objects into the right categories promotes hand-eye coordination and fine motor control.

• Focus and Patience: Sorting activities require concentration and the ability to work through tasks without rushing.

Materials Needed (Consider listing options):

• A variety of shapes and sizes of objects (such as blocks, buttons, or paper cut-outs)

• Sorting trays or bins (to separate shapes and sizes)

• Labels or colored stickers for categories (e.g., circles, squares, and triangles for shapes; small, medium, and large for sizes)

• Optional: Picture cards or flashcards with different shapes and sizes for reference.

Step-by-Step Instructions:

1. Prepare the Sorting Items:

• *Parent's Prompt: "Look at all these objects! We've got so many shapes and sizes. Can you help me sort them into different groups?"*

• Gather a collection of objects that come in various shapes and sizes, such as different kinds of buttons, blocks, or toys.

2. Set Up Sorting Categories:

• *Parent's Prompt: "Let's start by putting the round ones together. Do you think we can also sort them by their size?"*

• Set up trays or areas on the floor, labeling them with the categories you'll be using (shapes and sizes). You can also add labels for shapes like circles, squares, and triangles, and sizes like small, medium, and large.

3. Sort by Shape:

• *Parent's Prompt: "Let's begin with shapes! Can you find all the circles and put them in this tray?"*

• Help your child look for objects that match the designated shape categories and place them in the corresponding bins or areas.

4. Sort by Size:

• *Parent's Prompt: "Now let's sort these shapes by their size. Which ones are big? Which ones are small?"*

• After the shapes are sorted, encourage your child to organize them by size–small, medium, and large.

5. Combine Both Sorting Categories:

• *Parent's Prompt: "Let's see how fast we can sort both shapes and sizes at the same time. Can you put the small circles here and the big squares there?"*

• For a greater challenge, combine both sorting categories. Ask your child to sort by both shape and size simultaneously.

6. Reflect on the Sorting:

• *Parent's Prompt: "Great job! Let's take a look at all the piles we've made. Which pile was the biggest? Which one was the smallest?"*

• After finishing the sorting, reflect together on the experience. Discuss which categories were easier to sort and which ones required more attention.

7. Reorganize and Try Again:

• *Parent's Prompt: "Let's mix up the shapes again and sort them one more time! Can you do it faster this time?"*

• For further practice, jumble up the objects and sort them again, seeing if your child can do it more quickly or accurately.

Reflective Questions to Deepen the Experience:

- *"Which shape was your favorite to sort? Why?"*
- *"How did you know which objects were small, medium, or large?"*
- *"Do you think some shapes fit into more than one category?"*
- *"What makes a circle different from a square?"*
- *"Can you think of any other things around the house that fit these shapes or sizes?"*
- *"Which group had the most items? Which one had the fewest?"*
- *"What happens if we sort shapes by color instead of size?"*
- *"How do shapes and sizes help us understand how things fit together?"*
- *"Why do you think it's important to sort things into categories?"*
- *"Could we make a game where we sort things by both shape and size, but also speed?"*

Bonus Challenges or Variations:

• Speed Sorting: Challenge your child to sort all the items as quickly as possible. Can they beat their previous time?

• Shape and Size Memory Game: After sorting, mix the items up and play a memory game where your child needs to remember where specific shapes or sizes were placed.

• Sorting by Color: Add another level of complexity by including a color sorting challenge in addition to shape and size.

• Pattern Creation: Once sorting is complete, encourage your child to create patterns with the sorted objects (e.g., circle, square, circle, square).

Why This Activity Matters:

Shape and Size Sorting is a perfect way to engage your child in developing early cognitive and motor skills while having a lot of fun! This activity encourages logical thinking and reinforces how we observe and categorize the world around us. Through sorting, children learn important lessons in organization and classification that will serve as a foundation for more complex tasks in the future.

8. MUSICAL MEMORY

Objective:

Musical Memory is a fun and interactive game that helps children improve their listening, memory, and concentration skills through music. In this activity, children will play memory-based games using simple tunes and sound patterns, making it an enjoyable and educational experience. They will also explore rhythm, pitch, and timing while engaging in creative play.

Activity Overview:

In Musical Memory, children listen to a variety of musical sounds, from simple tunes to rhythmic patterns, and then try to remember and repeat them. This activity not only enhances memory skills but also strengthens their musical ear, improving auditory discrimination and the ability to follow patterns. It's a great way to bond over music while learning!

What Your Child Learns from This:

• Memory and Recall: The game strengthens memory retention and recall by encouraging children to remember specific sounds and patterns.

• Listening Skills: Children develop the ability to listen attentively, focusing on musical tones, rhythms, and melodies.

• Musical Awareness: It introduces children to basic musical concepts such as rhythm, pitch, and melody.

• Concentration: The game helps improve focus and attention as children work to remember musical patterns.

• Creative Expression: Children may have opportunities to create their own musical patterns, fostering their creativity and musical imagination.

Materials Needed (Consider listing options):

• Instruments or Sound Makers: You can use musical instruments (like a xylophone, tambourine, or bell), pots, pans, or even clapping hands.

• Recording Device or Music Player: A way to play recorded musical patterns or tunes (optional).

• Paper and Crayons: For drawing patterns or writing down notes, if your child likes to visualize music.

• Timer or Stopwatch: To add a time challenge to the activity.

Step-by-Step Instructions:

1. Set Up the Musical Challenge:

• *Parent's Prompt: "Let's play a game where you listen carefully to the sounds I make. Can you remember them and repeat them back to me?"*

• Prepare a set of instruments or sounds to use. You can choose easy-to-remember patterns to start, gradually increasing complexity.

2. Play a Musical Pattern:

• *Parent's Prompt: "Here comes the first sound–listen closely! Tap-tap-tap... What do you think that sounded like?"*

• Tap a rhythm, play a simple melody, or create a sound pattern using instruments or clapping.

3. Ask Your Child to Repeat:

• *Parent's Prompt: "Can you copy that sound? Try tapping it just like I did!"*

• Allow your child to try to replicate the pattern they just heard, encouraging them to listen and repeat it.

4. Increase the Challenge:

• *Parent's Prompt: "This time, I'm going to play three sounds in a row. Can you remember all of them?"*

• Gradually increase the number of sounds or notes in each sequence, making the game more challenging as your child improves.

5. Create Your Own Patterns:

• *Parent's Prompt: "Now it's your turn! Can you make a sound pattern and see if I can remember it?"*

• Encourage your child to create their own patterns using instruments or clapping, while you try to remember and repeat them.

6. Reflection Time:

• *Parent's Prompt: "Great job! What was the hardest part of remembering the pattern? What helped you remember the sounds?"*

• Discuss how they felt about the game and what strategies they used to recall the sounds.

Reflective Questions to Deepen the Experience:

- *"What helped you remember the pattern? Was it the rhythm, the sounds, or something else?"*
- *"How did it feel when you could copy the sound back perfectly?"*
- *"Can you think of other sounds we could use in the game? What other instruments might work?"*
- *"How can we make the patterns even harder? Should we add more sounds?"*
- *"Did you find it easier to remember the patterns with certain instruments or sounds?"*
- *"What would you name the sounds we just created? Could they be part of a song?"*
- *"How did listening carefully help you in the game?"*
- *"What was the trickiest pattern to remember? How did you solve it?"*
- *"Can you think of a fun rhythm we could use in another game?"*
- *"How do you think musicians remember and play complex music?"*

Bonus Challenges or Variations:

• Tempo Challenge: Change the tempo of the patterns. Start slow and gradually increase the speed to see how quickly your child can replicate the pattern.

• Sound Exploration: Explore sounds from different environments (nature sounds, household sounds, etc.) and incorporate them into the game.

• Rhythm and Melody Combination: Combine rhythm with melody (e.g., a pattern of claps followed by a musical note or tone) to make the challenge even more engaging.

• Create a Musical Story: After practicing patterns, ask your child to build a musical story with their own sequences of sounds, and have them tell a story while you play the sounds that match their narrative.

• Group Play: Play the game with multiple children, and each child can add one element to the pattern, making the sequence more complex as the game progresses.

Why This Activity Matters:

Musical Memory is an engaging activity that enhances a child's auditory skills, concentration, and memory in a fun, interactive way. By using music as a tool, this game nurtures children's cognitive and musical development, allowing them to grow their attention span and memory while having a blast!

9. TREASURE HUNT WITH CLUES

Objective:

Embark on an adventure with your child by creating a fun and interactive treasure hunt that enhances their critical thinking, problem-solving, and teamwork skills. By following clues and deciphering riddles, children will engage in imaginative play while developing a deeper understanding of how to break down challenges and think critically to reach a goal.

Activity Overview:

Treasure hunts are timeless adventures that blend fun with learning. This activity involves creating a treasure map or a series of clues for your child to follow, each step bringing them closer to the ultimate treasure! As they work to solve each clue, children practice reading comprehension, reasoning, and exploration, all while enjoying the thrill of discovery.

What Your Child Learns from This:

• Problem-Solving: Decoding clues and overcoming challenges teaches critical thinking and strategy.

• Teamwork: If you decide to participate together, this activity can strengthen your child's collaborative and communication skills.

• Following Directions: Your child will practice listening and interpreting instructions accurately.

• Spatial Awareness: Moving from one clue to another helps your child navigate their environment and strengthen their understanding of directionality.

• Patience and Persistence: It takes time to solve each clue and move forward in the hunt, encouraging your child to stick with problems until they find solutions.

Materials Needed (Consider listing options):

• Clue Cards or Paper: For writing the clues. You can make them decorative or thematic for added excitement.

• A "Treasure" item: This could be a small toy, treat, or token that's special to your child.

• Pens or markers for drawing a map or writing clues.

• Envelopes or boxes to hide the clues.

• Stamps, stickers, or small treasures to leave with each clue.

• Optional: Small props to make each clue location more exciting (e.g., a pirate hat, magnifying glass, or pretend map for a pirate treasure hunt theme).

Step-by-Step Instructions:

1. Plan the Treasure Hunt:

• *Parent's Prompt: "We're going on a treasure hunt today! But first, we need to decide where the treasure is hidden and what clues will lead us to it. Let's think about the adventure we want to create!"*

• Decide on the treasure location and map out where you'll hide the clues. Each clue should lead to the next, with the final clue revealing the treasure.

2. Create the Clues:

• *Parent's Prompt: "Clues can be tricky, so let's make sure they're just the right level of challenge. You can write riddles, give hints about where to go next, or even draw pictures!"*

• Write or draw your clues on small pieces of paper. You can make the clues rhyming riddles, puzzles, or simple directions. For example, "I'm green and tall, with leaves in the air, look underneath me, and you'll find something rare."

3. Set the Stage:

• *Parent's Prompt: "Now, let's hide the clues! We'll put them in places that your child knows well, but they'll still have to think carefully to figure out where they are!"*

• Hide each clue in its designated spot. Make sure that the clues aren't too difficult for your child to find but still pose a fun challenge.

4. Give the First Clue:

• *Parent's Prompt: "Here's your first clue! Let's see if you can follow it to the next one. Remember, every clue brings you closer to the treasure!"*

• Present your child with the first clue and let them begin the hunt. If they need a little help, you can offer gentle hints to keep the hunt moving.

5. Follow the Trail:

• *Parent's Prompt: "You're doing great! Now, let's see where the next clue leads. Keep your eyes open—some clues might be tricky!"*

• Help your child follow each clue and move from one location to the next. Along the way, celebrate their problem-solving skills and curiosity.

6. Uncover the Treasure:

• *Parent's Prompt: "Wow, you did it! You found the treasure! What's inside? Can you describe it and imagine a fun story about it?"*

• Once your child finds the treasure, celebrate the victory together! Open the box or envelope to reveal the prize and reflect on the journey.

7. Reflect and Discuss the Hunt:

• *Parent's Prompt: "What part of the treasure hunt was the most fun? Was there a clue that was tricky? What did you do when you got stuck?"*

• Ask your child to reflect on the clues and their journey, encouraging them to think about what worked well and what could be improved in the future.

Reflective Questions to Deepen the Experience:

- *"What was your favorite clue? Why?"*
- *"How did you feel when you solved a tricky clue?"*
- *"What did you learn from following the clues?"*
- *"If you had to hide a clue for someone else, where would you hide it?"*
- *"What could the treasure be used for? What story would you tell about it?"*
- *"What would you do differently if you had to create your own treasure hunt?"*
- *"How did you keep track of the clues? Did you follow them step-by-step or did you guess?"*
- *"Why is it important to pay attention to all the clues?"*
- *"What would have happened if you missed one clue? How did you solve it?"*
- *"If we went on another treasure hunt, what kind of treasure would you want to find?"*

Bonus Challenges or Variations:

• Theme It! Make your treasure hunt even more exciting by adding a theme. A pirate treasure hunt, a jungle adventure, or a space mission could add layers of fun and imagination.

• Incorporate Physical Challenges: Some clues could require physical tasks, like jumping five times or spinning around before they can continue.

• Interactive Clues: Use riddles that involve solving a puzzle or decoding a message (e.g., a simple cipher or picture-based clue).

• Multiple Treasure Hunts: Set up different routes or have multiple treasures hidden for a more extended challenge.

Why This Activity Matters:

Treasure Hunt with Clues is an exciting way for children to sharpen their problem-solving, reasoning, and teamwork skills —all while having a blast. By leading them on a thrilling adventure, you help foster a love of exploration and learning. Whether they're decoding clues, following a map, or imagining a story behind the treasure, your child will feel a sense of accomplishment and joy as they complete the hunt!

10. DIY MEMORY BOOK

Objective:

Create a personalized memory book with your child to capture special moments, fostering both creativity and reflection. This activity will help children practice storytelling, fine motor skills, and emotional expression, while creating a keepsake that they can treasure forever.

Activity Overview:

In this activity, your child will create their own DIY memory book by filling it with pictures, drawings, and mementos of memorable experiences. Together, you will brainstorm and organize the pages to reflect your child's most cherished memories. As they choose photos, draw scenes, and write about their experiences, they will practice important skills like sequencing, storytelling, and visual arts, all while bonding with you over the creation of something uniquely theirs.

What Your Child Learns from This:

• Storytelling Skills: Organizing memories and experiences into a book teaches children the art of narrative. They'll learn how to sequence events and express thoughts clearly.

• Emotional Expression: Reflecting on and recording special moments helps children understand and express their emotions.

• Fine Motor Skills: Cutting, pasting, and drawing develop fine motor coordination.

• Creativity: Decorating pages, choosing materials, and designing the layout encourage artistic expression and creativity.

• Organizational Skills: Arranging memories into a book helps children practice organizing thoughts, photos, and mementos.

Materials Needed (Consider listing options):

• Blank notebook or scrapbook (or sheets of paper to bind into a book)

• Markers, crayons, and colored pencils

• Photographs or printed pictures (you can print photos from a family trip or events)

• Stickers, stamps, and embellishments (for decoration)

• Glue, tape, and scissors

• Ribbons or string (for tying up the book or adding a creative touch)

• Optional: Special mementos like ticket stubs, postcards, or drawings

Step-by-Step Instructions:

1. Prepare the Memory Book Base:

• *Parent's Prompt: "We're going to make a memory book! We'll fill it with pictures, drawings, and all the wonderful moments we've shared together."*

• Set up a blank notebook or scrapbook as the base of the book.

2. Pick a Theme or Timeline:

• *Parent's Prompt: "What's the first memory we should put in our book? Maybe a favorite family vacation or a birthday?"*

• Decide on a theme for the book or create a timeline of significant events, such as milestones, favorite holidays, or adventures.

3. Select and Add Photos or Drawings:

• *Parent's Prompt: "Let's pick out some pictures that remind us of happy times. Which ones do you want to include?"*

• Let your child choose photos or draw scenes that represent the special memories. Encourage them to talk about what each memory means to them.

4. Write About the Memories:

• *Parent's Prompt: "Can you tell me what happened in this photo? Let's write a sentence or two about it."*

• Help your child write captions or short descriptions of the memories, including emotions or funny details.

5. Decorate the Pages:

• *Parent's Prompt: "Let's make this page even more special with some stickers or doodles. How should we decorate this memory?"*

• Encourage your child to decorate the pages with stickers, stamps, or drawings that reflect the theme of each memory.

6. Bind or Organize the Book:

• *Parent's Prompt: "Now that we've filled the pages, let's make our memory book look really nice! Should we tie it up with ribbons or leave it open like a scrapbook?"*

• Bind the pages together, or create a hardcover if using loose pages.

7. Reflect on the Process:

• *Parent's Prompt: "Look at all the memories we've captured in our book! How do you feel about looking back at these special moments?"*

• After finishing the book, talk with your child about what they've created and how it makes them feel.

Reflective Questions to Deepen the Experience:

- *"Which memory was the most fun to put in the book?"*
- *"How did you feel when you saw the photos? Did any of them make you smile?"*
- *"What memory is your favorite? Why?"*
- *"Can you think of another event we could add to the book? What's something you really enjoyed?"*
- *"What emotions do you feel when you look at your finished book?"*
- *"Do you think this memory book will help you remember all the fun things we did?"*
- *"What would you add to the book if we went on another adventure?"*
- *"Which part of the book do you love the most? Is there a page you want to show others?"*
- *"How do you think we can keep making more memories like this?"*
- *"How did you feel when we talked about these memories together?"*

Bonus Challenges or Variations:

• Add a Family Tree Section: Include a page for your child to draw a family tree, adding photos or illustrations of family members and their relationships.

• Seasonal Pages: Create a memory book that highlights each season–spring adventures, summer vacations, fall holidays, and winter festivities.

• Memory Jar: In addition to the memory book, create a memory jar. Have your child write down moments they want to remember and add them to the jar. Over time, this can serve as a collection of fond memories.

• Special Messages: Add pages where family members can write messages to your child. Over time, this could become a cherished collection of loving words.

Why This Activity Matters:

The DIY Memory Book offers a wonderful way to preserve special memories while fostering creativity, emotional development, and storytelling. It allows your child to reflect on their experiences, enhancing their ability to express emotions and gain a deeper understanding of the world around them. What a meaningful keepsake to cherish for years to come!

3. Problem-Solving Skills

P roblem-solving is a foundational life skill that helps children approach challenges with creativity, logic, and perseverance. In this chapter, you'll discover activities designed to stimulate critical thinking, encourage experimentation, and foster resilience in your child. Through these playful yet purposeful exercises, children will learn how to analyze situations, explore solutions, and embrace mistakes as opportunities for growth—all while building confidence and enjoying quality time with you.

"Difficulties are things that show a person what they are."

- Epictetus

1. ULTIMATE PUZZLE POWER-UP!

Objective:

Boost your child's problem-solving skills, creativity, and focus by engaging them in the world of puzzles! This activity helps enhance critical thinking while providing a sense of accomplishment as they solve intricate challenges.

Activity Overview:

Step into the realm of ultimate puzzle-solving! In this activity, your child will work with a variety of puzzles, from jigsaw puzzles to brain teasers, to activate their mental muscles. Along the way, they'll learn about perseverance, pattern recognition, and attention to detail. Whether they're assembling pieces or solving riddles, they'll feel like a puzzle master with each piece they fit together or answer they solve.

What Your Child Learns from This:

• Critical Thinking: Solving puzzles helps your child improve their reasoning and decision-making abilities.

• Attention to Detail: Assembling a puzzle or solving a riddle requires precision and the ability to notice small details.

• Perseverance: Puzzles often require patience. This activity teaches your child that it's okay to take time and try multiple solutions before finding the right one.

• Spatial Awareness: For jigsaw puzzles, children will develop a better sense of how pieces fit together and how to look for patterns.

• Self-Confidence: Successfully completing a challenging puzzle boosts self-esteem and reinforces the importance of persistence.

Materials Needed (Consider listing options):

• Jigsaw puzzles (varying difficulty levels)

• Brain teasers (word puzzles, Sudoku, or riddles)

• Puzzle timer (optional, for added excitement)

• Pen and paper (for sketching or solving riddles)

• Puzzle mat (for easy storage and reassembly of large puzzles)

• Printable puzzle templates (for creating personalized puzzles)

Step-by-Step Instructions:

1. Set the Puzzle Scene

• *Parent's Prompt: "We're about to become puzzle masters! Today, we're going to solve the biggest and coolest puzzles ever. What kind of puzzle do you think we'll solve first—one that challenges our brains, or one that's full of fun colors?"*

• Choose a puzzle that matches your child's ability level. Start with simple puzzles if they are younger, or try something more complex as they gain confidence.

2. Choosing the Right Puzzle

• *Parent's Prompt: "Let's pick a puzzle that'll challenge us today! Do you want to try a jigsaw puzzle with lots of pieces, or maybe a tricky riddle to solve?"*

• If you're doing jigsaw puzzles, decide on a small section to start with (e.g., corners or edges). For word puzzles or riddles, choose a fun brain teaser and encourage your child to think about how to break down the problem.

3. Puzzle Power-Up!

• *Parent's Prompt: "Ready to dive into this puzzle? Let's see if we can find the corners first. What do you think? Do the edges look like they'll fit together?"*

• As your child begins solving, encourage them to break the puzzle down into smaller tasks. For a jigsaw puzzle, focus on finding edge pieces first. If solving a riddle, ask them to start by looking for key clues.

4. Stay Focused and Keep Going

• *Parent's Prompt: "Great job! Keep going. If you get stuck, what could we try next? Maybe we need to look at the pieces from a different angle?"*

• Encourage your child to keep going even if they hit a roadblock. Remind them that puzzles are about persistence. If they're working with a timer, challenge them to beat their best time as they improve.

5. Reflect and Celebrate

• *Parent's Prompt: "We did it! Look at how far we've come. What do you think was the hardest part? How did we figure it out?"*

• Once the puzzle is complete, celebrate your child's achievement. This is a great time to discuss what they learned during the process and how it feels to complete a challenge.

Reflective Questions to Deepen the Experience:

• *"What was the hardest part of solving the puzzle? How did you feel when you finished?"*

• *"What do you think helped you solve this puzzle faster than the last one?"*

• *"If we added more pieces, how would we organize them? What strategy could we use?"*

• *"Why do you think puzzles are so fun? What do they make us think about?"*

• *"What do you notice about the pieces that fit together easily?"*

• *"How did you stay calm when the puzzle got tricky? Can you think of other times you've had to be patient?"*

• *"Do you think there's a pattern in how the puzzle pieces fit together? What do you look for?"*

• *"What would you do differently next time to make the puzzle easier?"*

• *"Could we make our own puzzle to challenge each other?"*

• *"How does it feel when a puzzle is really hard but you finally solve it?"*

Bonus Challenges or Variations:

• Timed Puzzle Race: Set a timer to see how fast you can solve a puzzle. Race against your child or each other to add a fun competitive twist!

• Puzzle Creation: Use printable templates or craft supplies to create your own puzzle for a personalized challenge. Draw a picture, cut it into pieces, and try to solve it together.

• Puzzle Variation: Try different types of puzzles, like word searches, Sudoku, or logic puzzles, to keep the brain active.

• Puzzle Relay: Create stations with different types of puzzles (jigsaw, crossword, riddles) and challenge your child to solve each one within a set time.

Why This Activity Matters:

By completing this activity, your child will strengthen their problem-solving skills and learn the value of persistence, patience, and critical thinking–all while having fun! This is a great way to introduce complex thinking in a fun and engaging way.

2. THE GREAT HIDDEN OBJECT QUEST!

Objective:

Engage your child in a fun and challenging treasure hunt activity that develops their observation skills, enhances their ability to focus, and promotes problem-solving, all while having an adventure to uncover hidden objects!

Activity Overview:

In this activity, you and your child will embark on an exciting quest to find hidden objects around the house, backyard, or any other safe space you choose. Each object represents a clue or part of a larger "treasure" puzzle. You can add themes, stories, and challenges to make it more immersive and educational. As your child solves riddles or completes challenges to uncover objects, they'll practice patience, attention to detail, and critical thinking.

What Your Child Learns from This:

• Observation Skills: The hunt requires your child to focus on their surroundings, identify clues, and notice small details.

• Problem-Solving: Your child will need to use logic and creativity to figure out where the objects are hidden and how to approach each challenge.

• Critical Thinking: As they solve riddles or puzzles to find the next object, they will be strengthening their thinking process and decision-making skills.

• Memory and Focus: Following clues or remembering previous objects found reinforces your child's ability to retain information and stay focused for an extended period.

Materials Needed (Consider listing options):

• Small toys or household items (anything you can hide!)

• Paper or notecards (to write clues, riddles, or instructions)

• Small bags or baskets (to collect found objects)

• Optional: Stickers, stamps, or drawings to decorate the treasure map or clues

• Timer (to add a challenge by limiting time for each clue)

Step-by-Step Instructions:

1. Set the Scene for the Quest

• *Parent's Prompt: "Today, we're going on a treasure hunt! There's something special hidden around the house that we need to find, and only the cleverest adventurers like you can uncover it!"*

• Choose a location for the hunt (indoor or outdoor). You could set up a treasure map with locations marked or draw a "trail" for your child to follow.

2. Prepare the Clues or Riddles

• *Parent's Prompt: "First, let's write down some clues to help us on our journey. Can you guess where the treasure might be hidden?"*

• Write clues or riddles that lead to different hidden objects. For example, "I'm something soft and fluffy, often found at bedtime. Where am I?" (Answer: Pillow). Or, "I have many colors and can be seen in the sky after a storm. Where can you find me?" (Answer: Rainbow-colored item).

3. Starting the Hunt

• *Parent's Prompt: "Are you ready for the first clue? Let's see if we can find this treasure together!"*

• Give the first clue or riddle to your child and let them figure out where to look. Celebrate their success when they find the first hidden object!

4. Continue the Quest with More Clues

• *Parent's Prompt: "Great job! Now, let's follow the next clue. Where might this object be hidden?"*

• After each object is found, provide the next clue leading to another hidden item. Keep the hunt exciting by making each clue a bit trickier than the last.

5. The Final Treasure Reveal

• *Parent's Prompt: "Here we are, the final clue! The treasure is so close, let's see what awaits us!"*

• The last clue should lead to a "treasure chest" or a box filled with fun rewards (toys, snacks, a special note, etc.).

6. Celebrate the Victory

• *Parent's Prompt: "You did it! You found all the treasures and completed the quest! How did you feel along the way?"*

• Ask your child how they felt during the hunt—were there any tricky parts, or did they feel like a true explorer? Talk about the adventure and let them share their thoughts on the experience.

Reflective Questions to Deepen the Experience:

- *"What was the most exciting part of the hunt?"*
- *"How did you figure out where to look for each object?"*
- *"Did any clues make you think hard? Which one?"*
- *"If you could create your own clue for a treasure hunt, what would it be?"*
- *"What made you feel proud during the quest?"*
- *"How did you feel when you found the last hidden object?"*
- *"Could you remember all the places we've already looked? How did that help us?"*
- *"If you could go on a real treasure hunt, what treasure would you want to find?"*
- *"What was your favorite clue or riddle?"*
- *"Would you change anything about the treasure hunt to make it even more fun?"*

Bonus Challenges or Variations:

• Timed Quest: Set a timer to see if your child can complete the quest in a certain time frame. This adds a challenge and helps them practice focus and speed.

• Treasure Map: Create a treasure map where your child follows a series of symbols or drawings that lead to each hidden object. This adds a visual element to the hunt.

• Team Challenge: If you have multiple children, make it a team competition to see who can find their items first or who can solve clues the fastest.

• Mystery Object: Hide a mystery object that your child needs to guess after finding it. Offer hints like "It's something you can wear" or "It makes noise when you play with it."

Why This Activity Matters:

This activity is a fun way for your child to practice important cognitive skills, like problem-solving, focus, and memory. By making the quest adventurous and imaginative, it also sparks creativity and storytelling, allowing them to feel like real explorers on a mission. You'll be helping your child build confidence and an ability to stay engaged and focused while having an unforgettable adventure together.

3. TOWER OF IMAGINATION

Objective:

This activity is designed to engage your child in a hands-on, creative experience that encourages problem-solving, critical thinking, and imaginative play. Through building and "destroying" towers, children will explore concepts of balance, structure, and construction, all while having fun!

Activity Overview:

In the Tower of Imagination, your child will construct towers using various materials, then have the excitement of knocking them down to see how the structure reacts. Through this activity, your child will learn about stability, trial and error, and creative design. Each time they build and destroy, they gain insights into cause-and-effect, spatial awareness, and the physical properties of different materials.

What Your Child Learns from This:

• Problem-Solving: Your child will experiment with different ways to make their towers stand taller or sturdier, using trial and error.

• Balance and Structure: They'll discover how balance works by stacking objects of different sizes and shapes to create stable or unstable towers.

• Spatial Awareness: As they build, they'll develop a better understanding of shapes, sizes, and how objects fit together.

• Cause and Effect: When knocking down their towers, they'll see the immediate result of their actions and learn the importance of structure and strength.

• Imagination and Creativity: The "destroy" part encourages dramatic play and storytelling, as your child might pretend to be a giant or a superhero.

Materials Needed (Consider listing options):

• Building blocks (e.g., wooden blocks, Legos, or toy bricks)

• Soft toys or figurines (to act as "giants" or "monsters" for the destruction part)

• Cardboard tubes (like paper towel or toilet paper rolls for extra height)

• Straws, sticks, or craft sticks (to reinforce structures or create towers with a different texture)

• Pillows or soft cushions (to provide a soft landing for tower destruction)

• Tape or glue (optional, if you want to make a more permanent structure before destruction)

Step-by-Step Instructions:

1. Set the Scene

• *Parent's Prompt: "Welcome to the land of giants and superheroes! We need to build the tallest tower to protect the kingdom. But beware, something might come along to knock it down!"*

• Encourage your child to use different materials (blocks, straws, tubes) to create a strong foundation for their tower. Ask them, "What do you think makes a tower tall and strong?"

2. Build the Tower

• *Parent's Prompt: "Let's start building! How can we make our tower as tall as possible without it falling over? What materials will you use to make it really strong?"*

• Your child can stack blocks, tubes, and toys in various ways. Talk through how the base needs to be wider for stability. Encourage experimentation with different heights and shapes to see which designs are the most stable.

3. The Destruction Challenge

• *Parent's Prompt: "Uh oh, here comes a giant or a monster! Let's see if your tower can survive the attack! What happens when we knock it down? Is it sturdy or does it fall over?"*

• Once the tower is built, encourage your child to knock it over—either by "attacking" it with soft toys or figurines, or by simply pushing it over. Watch how the different designs react. This is an opportunity to talk about balance, height, and structure.

4. Reflect and Redesign

• *Parent's Prompt: "What do you think made the tower fall? Could we make it stronger this time? Let's rebuild it with a new plan!"*

• Encourage your child to analyze why their tower fell or stayed standing, and then help them rebuild it with adjustments. Discuss how they can make it sturdier or taller.

5. Creative Destruction

• *Parent's Prompt: "This time, let's pretend we're a superhero or a giant. What's your special power that could destroy this tower? What else can we build to protect the kingdom?"*

• Introduce role-playing elements. Your child can act out different scenarios where they might destroy the tower (e.g., using a superhero punch or a giant stomp). This adds a creative layer to the physical aspect of the activity.

Reflective Questions to Deepen the Experience:

- *"Why do you think the tower fell when we did that?"*
- *"What could we change to make the tower stronger next time?"*
- *"If you were a giant, how would you destroy a tower? What would happen to the pieces?"*
- *"What makes a building or tower stay standing? What do we need at the bottom?"*
- *"What if we used a different material? Do you think it would be stronger?"*
- *"Can we build a tower that will stand against a really strong wind or a monster?"*
- *"What shapes do you think make the best towers?"*
- *"How can we make our tower even taller without it falling down?"*
- *"What's your favorite part of building the tower? What was the most fun part of knocking it over?"*
- *"How would you feel if you were the tower? Would you be scared of being knocked down?"*

Bonus Challenges or Variations:

• Team Tower Building: Have a family or friend team build a massive tower together, then take turns "destroying" it with soft toys.

• Survival Tower: Build a tower with extra challenge materials (e.g., tape, glue) and see if it can survive multiple "attacks" without falling.

• Nature Tower: If possible, take the activity outside and use natural objects like sticks, rocks, and leaves to build towers, exploring how different outdoor materials affect the structure.

• Towers for Animals: Create a special tower for stuffed animals or action figures to live in. Design the tower with them in mind, considering how strong or safe it needs to be for them to "live" inside it.

Why This Activity Matters:

This activity teaches children about the importance of trial and error in learning and building, while also giving them the freedom to be creative in both the construction and destruction phases. By reflecting on what worked and what didn't, your child will develop better problem-solving skills and a deeper understanding of how things work in the physical world. It's a fun, interactive experience that combines imagination with educational principles!

4. SUPER SORTING SPRINT!

Objective:

In this high-energy, fun-filled game, children will enhance their sorting, classification, and organizational skills while racing against the clock. The Super Sorting Sprint transforms learning into an exciting race, where kids practice sorting objects into different categories, boosting both cognitive development and motor skills!

Activity Overview:

Super Sorting Sprint turns sorting into an interactive and thrilling race. Your child will quickly classify objects by color, shape, size, or type, racing to beat the timer. This fast-paced, hands-on activity strengthens a child's ability to categorize and differentiate, while simultaneously helping them develop problem-solving skills and coordination. It's an activity that blends physical movement with mental challenge, making learning fun and exciting!

What Your Child Learns from This:

• Categorization Skills: By sorting different items into categories, your child learns about similarities, differences, and properties such as color, size, and shape.

• Speed and Focus: The race against the clock helps children develop time-management skills and the ability to focus under pressure.

• Motor Skills: Sorting objects and moving them quickly from one pile to another enhances hand-eye coordination and fine motor control.

• Problem-Solving: Children must figure out the most efficient way to complete the task, improving their problem-solving and critical thinking abilities.

Materials Needed (Consider listing options):

• A variety of small objects (buttons, coins, toys, or household items like pencils, blocks, etc.)

• Sorting bins or trays (one for each category)

• Labels or color-coded stickers for categories (e.g., red for shapes, blue for colors)

• Timer (either a kitchen timer or an app to track the time)

• Optional: For an added challenge, use objects with different textures or sizes to enhance sensory learning.

Step-by-Step Instructions:

1. Prepare the Sorting Items:

• *Parent's Prompt: "Let's get ready for a super sorting sprint! We've got our race items–blocks, buttons, and toys. Ready to see how quickly you can sort them into groups?"*

• Gather a variety of objects that can be sorted by different criteria, like color, shape, size, or type.

2. Set the Categories:

• *Parent's Prompt: "We're going to sort these into different piles. Let's think–what groups can we make? We can use shapes, colors, or even the size of the items!"*

• Label your sorting bins or create areas on the floor for each category.

3. Start the Timer:

• *Parent's Prompt: "Okay, the clock is ticking! You have one minute to sort these items. Can you do it faster than last time?"*

• Start the timer and encourage your child to sort the objects into the right categories as quickly as possible.

4. Race and Sort:

• *Parent's Prompt: "Go, go, go! Remember, focus on sorting each item as fast and accurately as you can."*

• As your child sorts, encourage them to think about their strategy and help them stay on task without rushing too much.

5. Check the Sorting:

• *Parent's Prompt: "Great job! Now let's see if everything is in the right place. You were really quick!"*

• After the timer goes off, check each pile to see if the objects are correctly categorized.

6. Reflect on the Sprint:

• *Parent's Prompt: "What did you learn while sorting? Was there a faster way to do it next time?"*

• Discuss with your child what went well, what could be improved, and how they can sort more efficiently next time.

7. Re-race:

• *Parent's Prompt: "Let's do it again! Can you beat your previous time or make the sorting even more accurate?"*

• Encourage your child to keep racing and refining their sorting skills by redoing the sprint with new objects or categories.

Reflective Questions to Deepen the Experience:

• *"What helped you sort faster this time?"*

• *"Which category was the hardest to sort? Why?"*

• *"How did you decide which pile the items should go into?"*

• *"What's the best way to organize objects? Can we try sorting by a different characteristic?"*

• *"Did you get faster as you went along? What made you quicker?"*

• *"What other items in the house could we use to make the sorting game even more interesting?"*

• *"Can you think of a way to make the sorting more challenging?"*

• *"What do you think will happen if we add more piles? Would it be easier or harder to sort?"*

• *"How do you think sorting objects helps you understand the world better?"*

• *"What new strategy can we try next time to improve your sorting time?"*

Bonus Challenges or Variations:

• Speed Sorting: Try to beat your own time or compete with family members to see who can sort the most objects in the least amount of time.

• Sorting by Multiple Categories: Increase the challenge by sorting items based on more than one category (e.g., sorting by both color and size).

• Sensory Sorting: Add sensory elements by including objects with different textures and letting your child sort them based on touch.

• Big vs. Small Challenge: Sort objects into "big" and "small" categories, or "light" and "heavy" categories for a different twist.

• Team Sorting: Partner up with your child to sort as a team! Each person can handle one category and see how fast you can both finish.

Why This Activity Matters:

Super Sorting Sprint is a perfect mix of physical activity and cognitive development. The excitement of racing against the clock keeps children engaged while they practice important skills like sorting, categorizing, and problem-solving. This activity is ideal for building focus and fine motor skills, while giving children a sense of achievement as they race to the finish line!

5. NATURE DETECTIVE ADVENTURE!

Objective:

In this adventure, children will become "nature detectives," using their powers of observation to explore the outdoors and solve nature-based mysteries. This activity nurtures their curiosity, fosters scientific thinking, and strengthens their ability to observe, classify, and investigate patterns in the natural world.

Activity Overview:

Nature Detective Adventure turns your backyard, local park, or nearby forest into an exciting detective's mission. Armed with a magnifying glass, notebook, and a keen eye, your child will explore the world around them and solve nature mysteries, like identifying animals, plants, or hidden objects. This adventure sharpens observation skills, encourages scientific inquiry, and strengthens a child's connection to the environment.

What Your Child Learns from This:

• Observation Skills: They will learn to notice small details in nature that are often overlooked.

• Critical Thinking: The detective theme encourages children to think critically about what they observe and make connections between their findings.

• Scientific Exploration: Engaging with the natural world through questioning, investigating, and classifying helps children develop early scientific skills.

• Curiosity and Imagination: The "detective" aspect of the activity stimulates curiosity and encourages a sense of wonder about the world around them.

• Patience and Focus: Tracking down clues and carefully examining nature requires patience and concentration, helping kids improve these skills.

Materials Needed (Consider listing options):

• Magnifying glass (to examine small details up close)

• Notebook and pencil (for taking notes, drawing findings, and solving clues)

• Camera or smartphone (optional, for capturing interesting discoveries)

• Binoculars (for spotting distant animals or plants)

• Nature Detective Kit (can include items like a compass, tweezers, or a plant guidebook)

• Optional: A nature-themed scavenger hunt list with clues (e.g., "Find a leaf with five points" or "Spot a bird with blue feathers")

Step-by-Step Instructions:

1. Prepare for the Adventure:

• *Parent's Prompt: "Ready to become nature detectives? We've got a mission to solve! Our job is to find out what kinds of plants and animals live in our backyard or nearby park. Let's get our tools ready!"*

• Gather all the necessary materials and discuss with your child what kind of "clues" you'll be looking for during your adventure.

2. Create a Detective's Notebook:

• *Parent's Prompt: "What will we need to remember on our adventure? Let's start by drawing a page in your notebook for each type of clue we'll look for. We can jot down observations or draw pictures of what we find!"*

• Encourage your child to design their detective notebook, making sections for different clues they might uncover, such as animal tracks, specific plants, or bugs.

3. Set Up the Scavenger Hunt (Optional):

• *Parent's Prompt: "We've got a scavenger list to help us on our quest. Our job is to find and check off each item. Let's see if we can complete it before the sun sets!"*

• Create a nature-themed scavenger hunt list, either with pictures or words, that includes things like "find a feather," "locate a spiderweb," or "spot a red flower."

4. Investigate and Explore:

• *Parent's Prompt: "We're on a mission! Let's search for clues around us. Remember, the smallest things could be the biggest discoveries!"*

• As you explore, encourage your child to use their magnifying glass, binoculars, or camera to get up close to objects. Ask them to observe textures, colors, and shapes carefully.

5. Record Your Findings:

• *Parent's Prompt: "What did you discover? Let's make sure to write it down and draw pictures so we don't forget. What do you think this leaf or bug is doing in its environment?"*

• Let your child jot down or draw what they find in their detective notebook. You can also take photos of interesting objects or creatures you come across.

6. Solve the Mystery:

• *Parent's Prompt: "What do you think these clues tell us? Can you figure out what type of animal made these tracks, or what kind of tree this leaf came from?"*

• Work with your child to piece together clues and try to solve the mysteries, such as identifying plants or animals, or discovering how the ecosystem works together.

7. Reflect on the Adventure:

• *Parent's Prompt: "That was fun! What did we learn today? What surprised you the most about what we found in nature?"*

• After the adventure, reflect with your child on the most exciting discoveries. Discuss what they learned and how it felt to be a nature detective.

Reflective Questions to Deepen the Experience:

• *"What do you think makes the leaves turn that color in the fall?"*

• *"Can you describe the texture of the bark? How is it different from the leaves?"*

• *"How do you think this bug survives here? What does it need to live?"*

• *"What did you notice about the flowers or trees in this area?"*

• *"How do you think the animals we found fit into this place?"*

• *"Why do you think plants need sunlight to grow?"*

• *"What clues helped you find the mystery creature?"*

• *"Can you identify patterns in the things we found? What do you think they mean?"*

• *"What would you do if you were a nature detective every day?"*

• *"What do you want to investigate next time? Are there other mysteries to solve?"*

Bonus Challenges or Variations:

• Tracking Animals: If you're in an area with animals, try to track them by their footprints or sounds. Use binoculars to observe animals without disturbing them.

• Create a Nature Map: Encourage your child to draw a map of the area where you're exploring, marking where different objects or creatures were found.

• Night-Time Adventure: Take your detective skills to a new level by investigating nature at night! Use a flashlight to look for nocturnal creatures, and observe how the world changes after dark.

• Group Exploration: Invite friends or family members to join the adventure and work together to solve nature mysteries as a team.

Why This Activity Matters:

Nature Detective Adventure is a fantastic way to combine outdoor exploration with hands-on learning. It helps children develop scientific skills, boosts their observational abilities, and deepens their connection with the natural world. Whether you're solving mysteries in your backyard or exploring a forest trail, this activity provides endless opportunities for discovery, creativity, and fun!

6. MYSTERY RIDDLES: UNLOCK THE FUN!

Objective:

 In this engaging activity, children will solve fun and
challenging riddles, using their critical thinking, language
skills, and problem-solving abilities. Mystery Riddles will
encourage your child to think outside the box, enhance their
vocabulary, and develop their reasoning skills in a playful and
interactive way.

Activity Overview:

Mystery Riddles is an exciting and brain-boosting challenge where children will listen to, read, and solve riddles. This activity enhances their ability to think logically, encourages active listening, and strengthens their language comprehension. The fun lies in both the puzzle-solving and the moments of eureka when the answer finally clicks into place!

What Your Child Learns from This:

• Critical Thinking: Riddles require children to think logically, analyze clues, and deduce the right answer.

• Language Skills: Decoding tricky words, phrases, and descriptions helps children improve their vocabulary and language comprehension.

• Problem-Solving: They'll practice creative thinking, discovering solutions by piecing together hints and knowledge they already have.

• Focus and Patience: Riddles often require multiple attempts and careful thinking, teaching kids perseverance.

• Listening Skills: They'll enhance their ability to pay attention to details and actively listen for important clues.

Materials Needed (Consider listing options):

- A list of mystery riddles (printed or written down)
- Pen and paper for your child to write down guesses or solve puzzles
- Timer (optional, for a timed riddle challenge)
- Props (optional, to visually aid the riddles–for example, a small box, toy, or object that relates to a riddle)

Step-by-Step Instructions:

1. Introduce the Challenge:

• *Parent's Prompt: "Welcome to the Mystery Riddle Challenge! Your brain will need to think fast and carefully to solve these tricky riddles. Are you ready for the first one?"*

• Briefly explain what riddles are: "Riddles are like puzzles for your brain. They give you clues and ask you to think of something, but it's not always obvious. We have to use our brains and imagination to figure it out!"

2. Start with an Easy Riddle:

• *Parent's Prompt: "Here's a simple one to get started: I'm tall when I'm young, and I'm short when I'm old. What am I?"*

• Read the riddle aloud or display it for your child. Let them think for a moment before offering their answer.

3. Solve and Discuss:

• *Parent's Prompt: "What do you think the answer is? Think about things that can change as they get older. Let's see if your guess is right!"*

• After your child guesses or after a few tries, provide the answer: "A candle!" Explain why it fits and how they used their thinking to find it.

4. Continue with More Riddles:

• *Parent's Prompt: "Great job! Let's move on to another one. Here's a trickier one: The more you take, the more you leave behind. What am I?"*

• Encourage your child to take their time, providing hints if necessary. Celebrate correct answers to boost confidence.

5. Incorporate Time Challenges:

• *Parent's Prompt: "Let's race the clock! Can you solve three riddles in under 3 minutes? Ready, set, go!"*

• Use a timer to add a sense of urgency, which helps your child focus and enhances the excitement of the activity.

6. Reflect and Talk About the Process:

• *Parent's Prompt: "That was great! What made you think of that answer? Were there any riddles that were tricky or fun?"*

• Reflect together on which riddles were the hardest and why, reinforcing the process of thinking through clues carefully.

Reflective Questions to Deepen the Experience:

- *"What made that riddle so tricky? Can you break it down?"*

- *"How did you figure out the answer to that one?"*

- *"What clues helped you the most in solving the riddle?"*

- *"Were there any riddles that you got wrong? What did you learn from them?"*

- *"How do you think solving riddles helps you with other problems?"*

- *"Can you think of a riddle that you can make up for me?"*

- *"Which riddle was your favorite and why?"*

- *"How can we make our own riddle game with even harder clues?"*

- *"What do you think is the best strategy when solving riddles?"*

- *"How does it feel when you finally get the answer?"*

Bonus Challenges or Variations:

• Create Your Own Riddles: After solving a few, challenge your child to come up with their own riddles for you or for the family to solve.

• Riddle Relay Race: Set up a riddle relay race, where you and your child take turns solving riddles one after another. Time yourselves to see who can solve more riddles in a set time.

• Use Props: Turn some riddles into interactive puzzles using everyday objects. For example, give clues related to a toy or a household item.

• Riddle Scavenger Hunt: Hide clues around the house, each leading to the next, where each clue is a riddle your child must solve to find the next location or prize.

Why This Activity Matters:

Mystery Riddles: Unlock the Fun! offers a captivating way for children to exercise their minds while having a blast. By solving riddles, your child will sharpen their language, logic, and problem-solving skills–while having fun with you as their riddle-solving partner!

7. BALLOON POP ADVENTURE!

Objective:

In this action-packed, lively game, children will engage in physical activity, creativity, and problem-solving as they race to pop balloons in a series of exciting challenges. Balloon Pop Adventure not only gets kids moving, but it also nurtures teamwork, coordination, and strategic thinking while offering plenty of laughs along the way!

Activity Overview:

Balloon Pop Adventure is an energetic and thrilling game where children pop balloons using different techniques and solve fun puzzles to unlock challenges. Whether they are using their hands, feet, or creative thinking, this activity is sure to bring lots of excitement and laughter. With each balloon pop, your child enhances motor skills, learns about cause and effect, and participates in a hands-on experience that promotes active learning.

What Your Child Learns from This:

• Motor Skills: Whether popping balloons by jumping on them or using their hands, children practice hand-eye coordination, balance, and motor control.

• Problem-Solving: Each challenge or game variation requires your child to think creatively and develop strategies to complete the task.

• Teamwork: If playing in a group, your child will practice collaboration, communication, and working together toward a common goal.

• Cause and Effect: By engaging with the balloons and understanding how force, timing, and movement affect outcomes, your child learns basic physics concepts.

Materials Needed (Consider listing options):

• Balloon pack (latex or foil balloons in various colors)

• Inflation tool (air pump or breath for manual inflation)

• Markers, stickers, or glitter (for decorating balloons and adding excitement)

• String or ribbon (for tying balloons to secure spots)

• Paper or plastic cups (for some challenges, like using them to pop balloons)

• Timer or stopwatch (for timed challenges)

• Optional: Small treats or prizes to put inside the balloons for added surprise.

Step-by-Step Instructions:

1. Inflate the Balloons:

• *Parent's Prompt: "Time to start the adventure! Let's blow up our balloons and get them ready for popping! What colors do you want to choose for our balloons?"*

• Inflate the balloons and scatter them around the play area, or tie them to different spots where your child can easily reach them.

2. Prepare the Challenges:

• *Parent's Prompt: "What kind of challenge should we do today? Should we pop them with our feet or maybe race to pop the most in a minute?"*

• You can decide on the challenge, like popping with feet, popping using a spoon, or an obstacle course where your child needs to pop a balloon after completing a task.

3. Set Up the Adventure Area:

• *Parent's Prompt: "Let's create our adventure world. Maybe one balloon will pop when you jump on it, and another will need to be popped using a paper cup! How about we make a balloon jungle with all the different challenges?"*

• Set up an obstacle course or challenge area for popping balloons using various creative methods–using feet, hands, elbows, or spoons.

4. Race Against the Clock:

• *Parent's Prompt: "Ready, set, go! Can you pop this balloon before the timer runs out?"*

• Start the timer and encourage your child to pop the balloons using the specified method as quickly as possible.

5. Create a Balloon Puzzle:

• *Parent's Prompt: "Some balloons have surprises inside! Let's pop these and see what's hidden inside–are they tiny toys or candy?"*

• For added fun, put small surprises inside some of the balloons and encourage your child to figure out which balloons are special.

6. Challenge Variation:

• *Parent's Prompt: "What if we can only pop the balloons by jumping on them? Let's see who can jump the highest and pop the most!"*

• Vary the challenges by introducing different ways to pop balloons–like popping them by sitting on them, using a cup, or racing to pop as many as possible in a certain time.

7. Debrief the Adventure:

• *Parent's Prompt: "That was a wild ride! What did you enjoy the most? How did you pop the balloons? Let's talk about which balloons were the hardest and which were the easiest to pop."*

• After finishing the balloon popping fun, sit down and talk about the experience with your child.

Reflective Questions to Deepen the Experience:

• *"Which balloon was the hardest to pop? Why do you think that was?"*

• *"How did you feel when you popped a balloon?"*

• *"Do you think some methods of popping are faster than others? Why?"*

• *"What do you think makes a balloon pop–do you think the force matters?"*

• *"What was the most surprising thing you found inside a balloon?"*

• *"How did you feel when you completed a challenge?"*

• *"Can you come up with new ways to pop balloons?"*

• *"Why do you think the balloon popped when we did it this way?"*

• *"What if we tried popping balloons while doing jumping jacks– how would that change things?"*

• *"How can you be careful when popping balloons so they don't burst too suddenly?"*

Bonus Challenges or Variations:

• Obstacle Course Balloon Pop: Create a more elaborate adventure by making an obstacle course where your child must pop balloons at specific points.

• Team Balloon Pop: If playing with multiple children, create teams and see which team can pop the most balloons in a set time.

• Targeted Balloon Pop: Hang balloons at different heights, and challenge your child to pop the ones at the highest or farthest distance.

• Surprise Inside Challenge: Place small toys, stickers, or treats inside certain balloons for an extra surprise when they pop.

• Balloon Sculpting: Encourage your child to creatively shape and decorate balloons before popping them for an extra touch of artistry.

Why This Activity Matters:

Balloon Pop Adventure Extravaganza is a dynamic activity that stimulates physical movement, creative thinking, and problem-solving. The joy of popping balloons while racing against the clock, discovering hidden surprises, and overcoming challenges creates a memorable experience. Your child will build coordination, motor skills, and even teamwork, all while having tons of fun!

8. INDOOR OBSTACLE COURSE: NINJA STYLE!

Objective:

Transform your home into a ninja training arena! This action-packed activity is designed to improve your child's physical strength, coordination, balance, and agility while encouraging creative play. Children will love the challenge of navigating through an indoor obstacle course, testing their speed, dexterity, and problem-solving skills, all while having a blast!

Activity Overview:

Get ready to move and groove with an Indoor Obstacle Course that will turn your living room into an exciting ninja training ground! The course can be customized to suit your space and the items you have on hand. Your child will climb, crawl, jump, and balance their way through the course, honing their motor skills and enjoying a fun-filled physical challenge. Whether they're jumping over pillows, crawling through tunnels, or balancing on furniture, the ninja spirit will be alive in every twist and turn!

What Your Child Learns from This:

• Gross Motor Skills: Activities like crawling, jumping, and balancing help build core strength and coordination.

• Problem-Solving and Planning: Your child will need to think ahead about how to navigate each obstacle.

• Spatial Awareness: Moving through obstacles teaches your child about distance, depth, and body positioning.

• Focus and Determination: Staying focused to complete the course and mastering each obstacle builds persistence.

• Creative Play: The game encourages imaginative play as your child pretends to be a ninja in training, boosting creativity and storytelling.

Materials Needed (Consider listing options):

• Cushions or pillows (for jumping or crawling over)

• Chairs or tables (for crawling under or balancing on)

• Blankets or sheets (for creating tunnels or fort-like structures)

• Tape (for marking lines or setting up boundary areas)

• Hula hoops or small objects (for stepping through or over)

• Plastic cups or stackable toys (to build towers to knock down)

• Optional: Small cones or toys for target practice, yarn or string for a "laser" challenge.

Step-by-Step Instructions:

1. Set Up the Course:

• *Parent's Prompt: "Ready to become a ninja? Let's create your very own obstacle course! We can use pillows, chairs, and blankets–let your imagination run wild!"*

• Clear space in a room and gather your materials. Create a variety of obstacles: a pillow mountain to climb, a blanket tunnel to crawl through, or a chair balance beam to walk across.

2. Create Different Challenges:

• *Parent's Prompt: "What ninja moves do we need today? How about jumping over pillows, crawling through the tunnel, and balancing on the chair?"*

• Think about different challenges your child will love– climbing, balancing, crawling, jumping, and even throwing (e.g., knocking over stacked cups).

3. Designate the Start and Finish Line:

• *Parent's Prompt: "Let's start at this end of the room and race all the way to the finish line. You're going to be a real ninja in no time!"*

• Mark a clear starting point and finish line with tape, making sure your child knows the path they'll take.

4. Ready, Set, Go!

• *Parent's Prompt: "On your marks, get set, go! Can you jump from this pillow to that one without touching the ground?"*

• Have your child navigate through the obstacles, offering encouragement and cheering them on as they go.

5. Track Progress and Refine Moves:

• *Parent's Prompt: "Great job! You made it through the tunnel! Now, can you jump even higher next time, or balance longer on the chair?"*

• After each round, talk about what went well and suggest improvements or new challenges they can try to make it more difficult.

6. Race Against the Clock or Compete with a Partner:

• *Parent's Prompt: "Let's see if you can beat your time! How fast can you finish the course now?"*

• Time your child and encourage them to beat their personal best. If there's more than one child, they can compete to see who completes the course fastest.

7. Celebrate and Reflect:

• *Parent's Prompt: "You did amazing, ninja! What was your favorite part of the course? How did you feel when you completed it?"*

• Celebrate their accomplishments, and reflect together on the course. Discuss the challenges they faced and how they overcame them.

Reflective Questions to Deepen the Experience:

- *"Which obstacle was the hardest to complete? Why?"*
- *"How did you feel when you jumped over the pillows or crawled through the tunnel?"*
- *"What ninja skills do you think helped you get through the course?"*
- *"Which part of the course made you laugh the most?"*
- *"What other things could we use to make the course even harder?"*
- *"How can you improve your time next round?"*
- *"What did you do when you faced a difficult obstacle?"*
- *"If you were a ninja, what would your special power be?"*
- *"How do you feel when you finish the course? Excited? Proud?"*
- *"What would make the course even more fun or tricky?"*

Bonus Challenges or Variations:

• Ninja Precision: Add challenges where your child has to carefully pick up objects without dropping them or throw soft items into targets while navigating the course.

• Laser Maze: Use yarn or string to create a "laser maze" that your child must navigate without touching the "lasers" (the yarn).

• Team Ninja: If there are multiple children, create a relay race where they take turns navigating parts of the obstacle course.

• Timed Challenge: Race against the clock to complete the course as fast as possible and improve the time with each attempt.

• Ninja Stunts: Add a stunt section where your child can practice their "ninja flips" or a dramatic "jump from the top of the pillow mountain."

Why This Activity Matters:

The Indoor Obstacle Course: Ninja Style! is a perfect combination of physical activity and imaginative play. It encourages children to test their limits, strengthen their coordination, and think critically as they tackle obstacles. Plus, it's an engaging way to burn off energy indoors, creating lasting memories and helping your child feel like a true ninja warrior!

9. THE MEMORY MIX-UP ADVENTURE

Objective:

Get ready to put your memory and concentration to the test in this fun-filled adventure! This activity is designed to help your child enhance their memory, observation skills, and attention to detail. It's a playful, interactive way to challenge their brain and improve cognitive skills while having a great time. Let's dive into a world of memory games where items will magically appear and disappear, challenging your child to keep track and remember what's hidden!

Activity Overview:

The Memory Mix-Up Adventure is a memory-boosting game that's perfect for young children. With a set of everyday objects, you'll create a scene filled with surprises, then challenge your child to remember the sequence or the details of the objects in the game. They'll love the element of surprise as they try to recall what was where and what they saw. This activity helps improve short-term memory, attention, and focus while providing a good mental workout!

What Your Child Learns from This:

• Memory Retention: Your child will work on remembering details and recalling information in the correct order.

• Concentration: The game encourages focus and concentration as they observe and track changes.

• Critical Thinking: As the memory changes or items disappear, your child learns to think quickly and problem-solve.

• Observation Skills: The activity enhances their ability to notice and remember specific details.

• Social Interaction: If played with friends or family, it fosters healthy competition and collaborative learning.

Materials Needed (Consider listing options):

• A variety of small household items (toys, coins, buttons, pencils, etc.)

• A blanket or sheet (to cover and hide items)

• A timer or clock (optional, for timed memory challenges)

• Paper and pen (to write down the sequence for older children or to track the progress)

Step-by-Step Instructions:

1. Set Up the Memory Scene:

• *Parent's Prompt: "Let's get everything ready for our memory adventure! We'll use some of your favorite toys or objects for this game. I'll place them on the table, and you'll need to remember where everything is!"*

• Pick 5-10 objects and place them on a flat surface in a specific order. Make sure your child is looking closely at the objects before covering them up.

2. The Big Mix-Up:

• *Parent's Prompt: "Are you ready for the challenge? I'm going to cover everything with a blanket, and then we'll mix things up a bit!"*

• After a few seconds, cover the items with a blanket or cloth. While it's covered, secretly rearrange or remove a couple of items.

3. The Reveal:

• *Parent's Prompt: "Okay, let's uncover the objects and see what's changed! Can you remember what was there before? What's missing?"*

• Uncover the items and ask your child to identify what has changed or what has disappeared.

4. Memory Challenge:

• *Parent's Prompt: "Now that the items are mixed up, can you figure out where they were? Take your time and focus carefully!"*

• Let your child guess the order of the objects or recall the missing ones. For an added challenge, ask them to recall the sequence in which the objects were originally placed.

5. Progression and Variations:

• *Parent's Prompt: "What if we add more objects or make the scene even bigger? Can you remember a bigger set of items now?"*

• As your child becomes more skilled, increase the number of objects or add more complexity to the scene. You can also introduce time limits for a more competitive edge.

6. Reflection Time:

• *Parent's Prompt: "Great job, you remembered so much! What helped you remember? Was there anything you found tricky?"*

• After the game, talk with your child about their strategies and which items or parts were the hardest to recall. Praise their efforts and encourage them to keep practicing.

Reflective Questions to Deepen the Experience:

• *"What was the hardest part about remembering the items?"*

• *"How did you keep track of the objects in your head?"*

• *"What trick helped you remember what was there?"*

• *"Can you think of a different way to remember the sequence?"*

• *"What would happen if we added more objects–do you think it would be harder?"*

• *"How do you feel when you remember something that seemed impossible?"*

• *"What would you do if we played this game with your favorite toys?"*

• *"What helps you focus during this kind of game?"*

• *"How does your brain feel after playing this memory game?"*

• *"What other ways can we make this game more fun?"*

Bonus Challenges or Variations:

• Timed Memory Challenge: Set a timer and give your child a certain amount of time to memorize the sequence before it's covered. The faster they recall the order, the better!

• Reverse Memory: After mixing up the objects, ask your child to describe where each item was, in reverse order.

• Memory Race: If there are two children, make it a race to see who can remember the most details from the mix-up.

• Increased Difficulty: Gradually introduce more complex items, different categories (e.g., colors, shapes, or types of objects), or longer sequences for older children.

Why This Activity Matters:

The Memory Mix-Up Adventure is a fantastic way to challenge your child's brain while having fun. It not only strengthens memory retention and focus but also encourages your child to use creative strategies to recall details and think critically. As your child improves, this game can evolve into a more advanced challenge, fostering cognitive development and boosting confidence along the way!

10. CRAZY STORY BUILDER!

Objective:

This creative activity invites children to become the master storytellers of their own wacky adventures. By adding silly twists and unpredictable elements, children will flex their imagination muscles and practice storytelling skills. Not only is this activity great for fostering creativity, but it also helps your child understand story structure, narrative flow, and character development while having an enormous amount of fun!

Activity Overview:

In Crazy Story Builder, children get to create a wild and unpredictable story with endless possibilities. With a set of unique and fun prompts, your child will weave together characters, settings, and events into a unique tale. It's all about thinking outside the box and letting the imagination run wild. This activity is perfect for sparking creativity, improving verbal skills, and teaching your child how to form coherent stories– all while being totally goofy and entertaining!

What Your Child Learns from This:

• Storytelling Skills: By developing characters, plots, and settings, children practice how to build a narrative from start to finish.

• Creativity and Imagination: Children's imaginations will take center stage as they dream up bizarre and funny scenarios.

• Sequencing and Organization: Constructing a logical flow of events helps children understand sequence and structure.

• Vocabulary and Expression: As they describe characters and settings, children will expand their vocabulary and practice expression.

• Problem Solving: When faced with story challenges, kids will learn to think on their feet and make connections in new ways.

Materials Needed (Consider listing options):

• Paper and markers (for drawing characters, settings, or key scenes)

• Story prompt cards (e.g., "A brave penguin in space" or "A talking tree with a secret")

• Dice (optional, to decide on certain elements like character traits or settings)

• Notebook (for writing down the story)

• Optional: A toy box filled with figurines (for using as characters or story elements)

Step-by-Step Instructions:

1. Introduce the Story Building Concept:

• *Parent's Prompt: "How about we make up our own wild adventure today? We can use all sorts of crazy ideas! Let's see where the story takes us."*

• Start by explaining that you'll be making up a story together, and each of you will add an element as you go.

2. Pick a Story Starter:

• *Parent's Prompt: "Let's begin by choosing a story starter. Should we start with a character, a place, or an event?"*

• Use a story prompt card or roll dice to decide on the basic idea. For example, you might get a "dragon" as your character, "a haunted mansion" as your setting, and "a hidden treasure map" as the event.

3. Create the First Piece of the Story:

• *Parent's Prompt: "What do you think happens first in our story? Does the dragon discover the mansion, or does the treasure map lead him to a hidden forest?"*

• Begin building the story together. Each person adds one sentence or idea at a time, building upon the previous person's contribution.

4. Add Fun and Unexpected Twists:

• *Parent's Prompt: "What if the dragon could talk, but only in rhymes? Or what if the treasure map is magical and keeps changing?"*

• Encourage your child to add quirky twists to the plot–like a character turning into a different animal or a setting shifting locations–to make the story even crazier and more fun.

5. Develop Characters and Settings:

• *Parent's Prompt: "What does the dragon look like? Can we draw him? Does he have any unusual powers?"*

• Discuss the characters in detail and build on their personalities. Let your child describe them in their own words and have fun with physical attributes, like the dragon having wings made of feathers or the talking tree wearing glasses.

6. Continue the Story:

• *Parent's Prompt: "Now that we have our dragon, let's see how he gets out of the haunted mansion. What happens next?"*

• Keep adding to the story in small parts, using each other's ideas to build a unique, ongoing narrative.

7. Wrap Up the Adventure:

• *Parent's Prompt: "How do we end this story? Does the dragon find the treasure? Does he make a new friend?"*

• Conclude the story together, making sure it ties back to the main conflict and provides a satisfying ending, even if it's a little silly.

8. Reflect on the Story:

• *Parent's Prompt: "What part of the story was your favorite? Would you change anything if we did it again?"*

• Discuss the finished story, asking what your child liked most and what they would add or change for next time.

Reflective Questions to Deepen the Experience:

- *"If you could change the story's ending, what would you do differently?"*
- *"What kind of character would you add next time? Maybe a funny robot or a superhero?"*
- *"Why do you think the dragon wanted to find the treasure? Was it to help someone, or for something else?"*
- *"If you could live in one of the places in the story, which one would you pick?"*
- *"What would your character do if they faced a challenge like the one in our story?"*
- *"How did your character change throughout the story? Did they learn anything?"*
- *"What did you enjoy most about creating this story?"*
- *"Could you think of a new twist to add to the story? Maybe the treasure has a surprise!"*
- *"How did the story make you feel? Was it funny, exciting, or maybe a little scary?"*
- *"What do you think would happen if we continued the story tomorrow?"*

Bonus Challenges or Variations:

• Story Sequels: Create a follow-up story based on the original adventure. How do the characters change or evolve after the first story ends?

• Dramatic Performance: Act out the story with toys or even your own voices and expressions to bring the tale to life.

• Collaborative Drawing: As the story progresses, draw scenes or characters together to illustrate the adventure visually.

• Story Swap: After completing the story, have your child tell the story back to you in their own words, adding new details and twists as they go.

• Themed Stories: Use specific themes, like outer space, underwater worlds, or time travel, to create more focused and imaginative adventures.

Why This Activity Matters:

Crazy Story Builder is a fantastic way to develop your child's creativity, storytelling abilities, and confidence. It's more than just making up a tale–it's about working together, problem-solving, and exploring new ideas. Each story becomes a treasure trove of memories and learning, all while having a great time. Get ready to unlock a world of endless adventures!

MORE WAYS TO PLAY, LEARN, AND GROW TOGETHER

Expand your child's growth with the other two books in **The Parent-Child PLAYBOOK** series:

• **The Parent-Child PLAYBOOK - Learning Activities for Healthy Body and Mind**

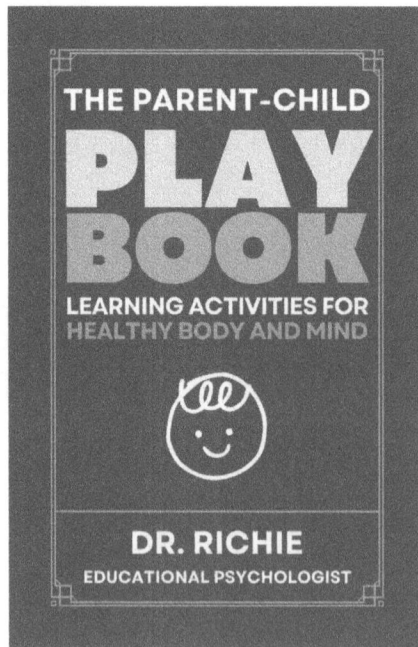

Help your child stay strong, healthy, and mentally focused with activities designed to balance the body and mind.

- **The Parent-Child PLAYBOOK - Learning Activities for Emotional, Social, and Communication Growth**

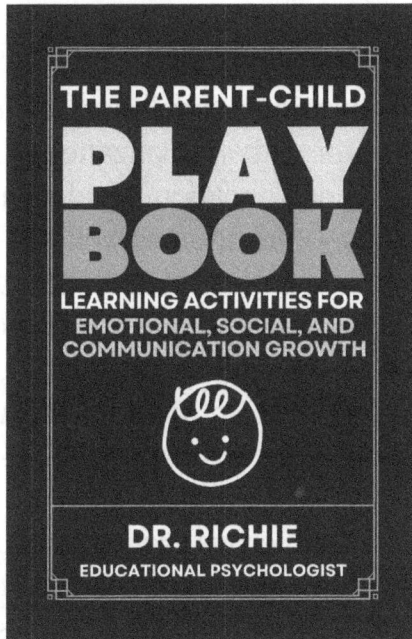

Focus on your child's emotional well-being and social interactions, providing them with the tools to build positive relationships and effective communication.

About the Author

Dr. Richie Kim is an educational psychologist and certified Early Childhood Educator with specializations in Infant-Toddler and Special Needs Education. Holding a teaching credential for elementary education as well, Dr. Richie has taught a diverse range of learners–from infants and toddlers to students with disabilities and graduate-level scholars. This extensive experience across schools, academies, corporations, and associations has provided Dr. Richie with a well-rounded, practical understanding of the educational landscape.

Dr. Richie has authored numerous academic papers and educational tools, including the WISE Learning Psychological Assessment, which has sold over 100,000 copies. As an award-winning entrepreneur, Dr. Richie is passionately dedicated to empowering families and educators through meaningful learning insights, guided by the mission: On a Mission to Impact Eternity through Learning Insights.

Dr. Richie seeks to transform lives by fostering stronger connections and creating lasting growth in children and their families.

The Parent-Child
PLAYBOOK
Learning Activities for Building a Creative Mind

Dr. Richie
Educational psychologist

www.ingramcontent.com/pod-product-compliance
Lightning Source LLC
Chambersburg PA
CBHW070021100426
42740CB00013B/2570